Identifying American Furniture

A Pictorial Guide to Styles and Terms
Colonial to Contemporary

THIRD EDITION, REVISED and EXPANDED

Milo M. Naeve

D1489105

W. W. NORTON & COMPANY
New York • London

Published in cooperation with the American Association for State and Local History

First Edition published 1981.
First Edition, second printing 1982.
Second Edition, revised and expanded 1989.

The original publication of this book was made possible in part by funds from the sale of the Bicentennial State Histories, which were supported by the National Endowment for the Humanities.

Distributed to the trade in the United States and Canada by:

W. W. Norton & Company
500 Fifth Avenue
New York, New York 10110

Printed in Canada.
1 2 3 4 5 6 7 8 9 0

LIBRARY OF CONGRESS CATALOGUING-IN-PUBLICATION DATA

Naeve, Milo M.
    Identifying American Furniture: a pictorial guide to styles and terms, colonial to contemporary / Milo M. Naeve. — 3rd ed.
        p. cm. — (American Association for State and Local History book series)
    Includes bibliographical references (p.   ) and index.
    ISBN 0-393-31844-3 (pbk.)
        1. Furniture—United States States—Styles. 2. Furniture—Expertising—United States.
I. Title. II. Series.
NK2405.N28 1998
749.213—dc21   97-33729
                                                                          CIP

Cover and Text Design: Gordon Chun Design
Editorial Management: AltaMira Press
Cover images courtesy of Art Institute of Chicago. Pieces described in detail in text.
See numbers 1, 50, and 130.

CONTENTS

ABOUT THE AUTHOR

MILO M. NAEVE is the Field-McCormick Curator Emeritus of American Arts at the Art Institute of Chicago. His responsibilities there were painting and sculpture to 1901 and decorative arts, including furniture, to the present. Naeve's articles and reviews have regularly appeared in the periodicals and journals devoted to American arts and culture. The Decorative Arts Society honored Mr. Naeve with the Robert C. Smith Award for the Most Distinguished Article in the Decorative Arts published in the United States in 1996.

Naeve was founding editor of the *Winterthur Portfolio* and edited the first three volumes. He is a member of the editorial board for *The American Art Journal,* a member of several honorary and professional societies in the United States, a trustee of the Skowkegan School of Painting and Sculpture, and, in England, a Fellow of the Royal Society of Arts. Naeve holds bachelor's and master's degrees in fine arts from the University of Colorado and the Winterthur Program of American Studies at the University of Delaware, respectively, and has lectured throughout the United States and in England. His book, *The Classical Presence in American Art,* released in 1978 by the Art Institute of Chicago, interprets the Classical influence on American art from the seventeenth century to the present. In 1978, the University of Delaware published Naeve's book *John Lewis Krimmel: An Artist in Federal America.* This artist, active from 1809 to 1821, founded the genre movement in American painting.

The three editions of Milo M. Naeve's *Identifying American Furniture,* first published in 1981 by the American Association for State and Local History, have become recognized as classic, compact guidebooks for identification of, and research on, American furniture.

INTRODUCTION

Distilling four hundred years of American furniture styles into one hundred pages of text is an optimistic effort. Omissions are necessary, and the compression holds grave potential for misunderstanding. But the need for identifying richly varied changes in American furniture, however crudely, is essential for introducing the general subject and offering guidance to specific issues. These considerations are the same as those fostering the book in 1981 as the first comprehensive survey of American furniture.

Two arenas for revision are commentaries about a style and examples of it. This edition even adds one style, the Empire. It is separated from the Classical styles, and that section is recast. The reason for change is the continuing enthusiasm for Classical interpretations that led in the last edition to withdrawing the Phyfe style from Classical styles. Division of the original category into three styles results in removing the now obsolete explanation in the original Preface, reprinted in the last edition, about the broad nature of the original Classical styles.

Since 1989, publications have increased greatly in number and offer significant new information. This surge is equally evident for furniture within the United States and elsewhere. Ever greater sophistication in documentation and analysis of it marks the movement. The new sources often cancel entries in the last bibliography or limit their usefulness. In this edition, as others, research of colleagues in documenting furniture illustrated in the text is noted in bibliographical references.

There is a comparable increase since the last edition in the quality of furniture and the number of examples publicly available. Illustrations are exclusively from them, as in earlier editions.

I hope the pace of discovering furniture and discovering information about it forces still another edition of *Identifying American Furniture.*

MILO M. NAEVE
Field-McCormick Curator Emeritus of American Arts
The Art Institute of Chicago

PREFACE

Styles in this handbook have swept nearly four centuries of designers, craftsmen, or patrons on the invisible winds of taste. They sometimes are an abrupt gale over a generation and sometimes a steady breeze over many.

I tried several times in several ways putting these constantly shifting and often elusive trends into a rational order in accordance with the first proposal for the project, made by Gary Gore, Director of Publications for the American Association for State and Local History. The Association wanted a succinct guide for identifying the style of a specific example, yet a broad survey for styles throughout our history. I declined.

The reasons are not mysterious. For one, the two objectives seemed contradictory. For another, I was greatly concerned at the time with very specific research on American paintings, and Gary's proposed project seemed to confirm a conclusion evident wherever curiosity erratically has led me, whether to the efforts of painters, sculptors, architects, silversmiths, potters, glassblowers, or cabinetmakers: Our knowledge of the past is incomplete. It is formed by the accident of survival for documentary evidence and for works of art coupled with the even more whimsical chance encounter with either source. A responsible survey in a distilled form seemed unlikely.

The idea haunted me, however, because I often came across the need for the kind of publication that AASLH proposed. Finally, we agreed on the venture. Like all fine publishers, mine is also a gambler. Gary has proven my greatest ally in giving complete freedom for translating his broad proposal into my specific approach. Our only foundation was that style, the appearance of furniture, is the most useful way of bringing clarity to a complex subject.

For that reason, the illustrations are the main elements of my survey. They are on the book's left-hand pages, for convenient reference, either for finding a style of interest or in comparing it with others for similarities or differences.

They are complemented in several ways. Superimposed numbers on each illustration identify stylistic elements that are listed on the right-hand page with a brief essay about the style. The overall number given to each picture (No. 1, No. 2, etc.) is a key to specific information in the illustration notes in the left column of the right-hand page.

A selection of periodicals, books, and articles in the section titled "Further Reading" completes the book. This section offers resources for specific inquiries from several points of view.

The user of this guide will find that looking through the illustrations is often the best kind of index, but the usual sort is included, listing the number of the illustrations where significant motifs, designers, craftsmen, manufacturers, materials, terms, and construction may be found.

Styles, then, are defined in this survey by the illustrations.

Each example is a fully developed expression, and, within a style, the selections offer elements that can be found in endless variations and combinations on other furniture. Elaborate interpretations of a style are emphasized, because their echo always remains in simplifications.

Especially before the mid-nineteenth century, styles evolved and lingered at different times in different places. My dates refer to the general period of popularity.

An individual would be best served, I decided, if all the furniture in the guide were publicly available. Owners are identified with the illustrations, but the listed sources are only a few of the many possibilities available to the reader in the United States and in England. I urge complementing this guide with a study of actual examples.

The greatest challenge in this survey has been to attain a balance between brevity and length. Styles have emerged in many different communities and areas that could be considered individually or treated as part of a broader trend. Most of my decisions are obvious. Others are personal, about the character of trends or the identification of trends that I believe will be useful to the greatest number of readers. There are, for example, separate categories for the Rococo Revival style and the Naturalistic style in the mid-nineteenth century: They are related, but they differ. What should be done with the styles of certain European immigrants? They often are the result of "folk" or "popular" culture, but I have separated them into Dutch, German, and Spanish traditions and excluded the distinctive French and Scandinavian furniture only because examples are few in number and less likely to concern the usual reader. Eccentric combinations of several styles are identified as "vernacular" styles, and examples were selected for demonstrating possibilities in the eighteenth and nineteenth centuries. I am uncomfortable with the term *vernacular,* which could refer to furniture in many degrees of simplification from sophisticated styles, but I prefer it to the inaccurate designation *country* and the vague one of *folk.* Windsor furniture may have originated with the generation of the Revolution, but it clearly is vital in our time, and I have taken the position of including a version with Windsors instead of Contemporary styles.

My names for styles usually are those in common use. They originated over the last century with the revival of designs from earlier periods and with an analytical approach to the history of furniture. Inconsistencies occur in references to political periods, design sources, craftsmen, religious or national groups, and international exhibitions, but the names have the advantage of general familiarity.

American furniture rarely can be mistaken for furniture made abroad, but Americans from the seventeenth century to the present have continued the international tradition of style launched by Greeks borrowing from Egyptians and Romans from Greeks. Among many influences, English taste prevailed through the seventeenth and eighteenth centuries, English and French in the nineteenth, and French and German in the twentieth. European books and magazines directly pertinent to the evolution of American styles are mentioned in the commentaries. Their significance is documented, but equally pertinent and rarely known specifically are the influences of immigrant craftsmen, imported furniture, and patrons traveling abroad.

Technology is considered in the guide mainly when essential to the visual features of style. At times, technology served craftsmen with better ways of manipulating materials or achieving decorative effects. At other times, it gave craftsmen such new materials as plastics. The influence of technology, however, should not be overestimated. An innovation, such as laminated woods, might be introduced in the mid-nineteenth century and ignored until the mid-twentieth.

The advantage of a summary in a handbook of this nature bears the counterweight disadvantage of omission.

Illustrations and text within these covers survey only major movements in domestic furniture. Many forms before the nineteenth century, especially bedsteads, have not survived for documenting styles completely. Innovative styles in the twentieth century are stressed over commercial adaptations and reproductions of historic styles, which are a fascinating dimension in cultural history but derivative in form and decoration.

A survey with a different accent could be published within a decade, if designers of contemporary furniture and researchers into the past continue their current vitality. But I believe my broad scheme is true now and will remain so for all who respond to the fascination of stylistic change through the years.

STYLES

1

2

3

4

5

6

Medieval Style, 1607–1700

1. Turned spindles
2. Stretcher
3. Splint seat
4. Finial
5. Trestle base
6. Chamfer
7. Moldings
8. Cleat
9. Chip carving
10. Egg-and-dart motif (Renaissance style)
11. Butterfly motif

English medieval traditions continue in New England and in the South through ordinary furniture in houses as sparsely furnished as those abroad. There is greater evidence for the appearance of storage and seating furniture than for bedsteads, settles, or livery cupboards.

The popular slab-ended chest is made of five pine boards nailed together, with sides extended as feet and a sixth board used as the pinned or hinged top. Decoration includes incised, punched, or painted geometric designs in red, black, brown, yellow, and white. The form occurs in England by the fourteenth century and continues in New England through the early nineteenth (No. 4).

Storage boxes are as simply made and decorated as chests. Some include chip carving, known in England by the thirteenth century but out of fashion there by the seventeenth century (No. 6).

Armchairs and side chairs with rush or splint seats and turned spindles, legs, and arms differ in design and kinds of woods used from New England to the South. These types of chairs occur as early as the eleventh century in England, but the usual English and American seat during the seventeenth century is the stool. Chair frames often were secured by shrinkage of unseasoned elements such as posts, around seasoned elements, such as arms and stretchers.

New England furniture includes a medieval type of a table with a removable top and stretcher on trestles. A version with a fixed top and stretcher continues to the early nineteenth century. Terminology of the period usually identifies the top as a "board" or "table" and the base as a "trestle." Tables of this kind were not stained or finished, because they were covered with a cloth (No. 2).

1. Armchair (Great Chair), Long Island or Connecticut, 1670–1710; ash. *The Art Institute of Chicago, Wirt D. Walker Fund, Chicago, Illinois.*

2. Table, New England, 1640–1670; pine top, oak base. *The Metropolitan Museum of Art, gift of Mrs. Russell Sage, 1909, New York, New York.*

3. Armchair (Great Chair), Virginia or North Carolina, 1690–1720; maple, oak. *The Museum of Early Southern Decorative Arts, Winston-Salem, North Carolina.*

4. Six-board Chest, Connecticut Valley, 1675–1725; pine. *Yale University Art Gallery, The Mabel Brady Garvan Collection, New Haven, Connecticut.*

5. Highchair for Child, probably Boston, Massachusetts, 1636–1670; silver maple. *The Art Institute of Chicago, gift of Elizabeth R. Vaughan, Chicago, Illinois.*

6. Box, New Hampshire, 1674–1700; white pine. Originally owned by Hannah (Mrs. James) Philbrick, 1656–1739. *The Art Institute of Chicago, gift of Marshall Field, Mrs. C. Phillip Miller, and Mrs. Frank L. Sulzberger, Chicago, Illinois.*

1
2
3
4
5
6

7

7
8

8

9
10
11

9

10

12
14
16
13
15
17
18
19

20
21
23
8
22

11

1. Finial (Restoration)
2. Strapwork
3. Relief carving
4. Grotesque
5. Foliate scroll
6. Ball feet missing
7. Doric column
8. Collarino (astragal molding)
9. Split spindle
10. Lozenge
11. Boss
12. Cleat
13. Stile
14. Rail
15. Stipple background on carved panel
16. Lunette
17. Muntin
18. Leaf design
19. Wooden pins secure mortise-and-tenon joint
20. Channel molding
21. Apron or skirt
22. Ball foot variation
23. Pendant

Rectilinear oak forms with boldly curved elements and massive turnings are accented with relief carving against backgrounds stained or painted black, white, green, and red. Survivals in the style of somber Renaissance splendor mainly are from New England.

Joiners secured parts with wooden pins or nailed bottoms and backboards. Chests and boxes are common among the limited forms. Seating includes joint stools—a reference to joined construction—and chair-tables with backs lowering for table tops. Court cupboards offer a bottom shelf below a recessed cupboard; press cupboards are a variation with compartments enclosing the lower section. Tables occasionally include leaves, either drawing outward or opening onto a moveable leg. Drawers are introduced, though rare. Evidence is limited for bedsteads, but they probably were similar to the nineteenth-century vernacular form, and elaborate versions apparently included posts.

The Renaissance style originated in England from continental versions of the Italian Renaissance. Revived from Roman art are acanthus leaves and flowers, Doric columns, Roman arches, and torus, scotia, and astragal moldings. They merge with Renaissance circular and round feet, channel moldings, bands of notches and triangles, bulbous turnings, lunettes, foliage, attenuated leaves, bosses, grotesques, lozenges, and strapwork. Spindles, cut in half, glued together, turned, and broken apart, form the common decoration known as "split spindles."

7. Armchair (Great Chair), Thomas Dennis (attributed), Ipswich, Massachusetts, 1668–1675; oak. *The Essex Institute, Salem, Massachusetts.*

8. Joint Stool, Stephen Jaques (attributed), Newbury, Massachusetts, 1681–1710; red oak. *The Henry Francis du Pont Winterthur Museum, Winterthur, Delaware.*

9. Press Cupboard, the Emery Shops (attributed), Newbury, Massachusetts, 1676–1695; oak, pine. *The Museum of Fine Arts, Boston, gift of Maurice Geeraerts, in memory of Mr. and Mrs. William R. Robeson, Boston, Massachusetts.*

10. Chest, Plymouth, Massachusetts, area, probably 1641 (dated); white oak, pine top. *The Art Institute of Chicago, Elizabeth R. Vaughan Fund, Chicago, Illinois.*

11. Table, Massachusetts, 1661–1690; oak. *The Wadsworth Atheneum, Wallace Nutting Collection, gift of J. Pierpont Morgan, Hartford, Connecticut.*

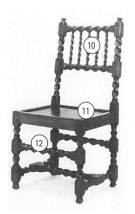

1. Cleat
2. Split spindle (Restoration)
3. Black paint
4. Owner initials
5. Reel turning
6. Ball foot variation
7. Cyma reversa molding
8. Astragal molding
9. Ovolo molding
10. Spiral turned spindles
11. Recessed seat for cushion
12. Stretchers (front, back, side, medial)
13. Bevel
14. Boss
15. Leather upholstery with brass tacks
16. Velvet cushion
17. Ball turning

Comforts and conveniences still known today are introduced in new forms featuring upholstery in couches, side chairs, or armchairs; drawers in tables, chests of drawers, or high chests; and tables with hinged leaves supported on gate-legs. Design and decoration of these forms shift radically from rectilinear simplicity at the close of the austere British Commonwealth in 1659 to Baroque curves with restoration of the monarchy and luxury. Innovations in form and decoration reached New England and the Middle Colonies over the late seventeenth century, often influenced the Renaissance Style, and merged into the later William and Mary Style.

Oak is common, but walnut and maple better serve the new fashions. Turnings range from round or oval shapes to discs or spirals. Feet are circular, round, or oval. Geometric panels on case furniture or drawers are framed by classical moldings or wide bevels against a field in light and dark woods, black and red paint, or grained patterns.

12. Chamber Table, Essex County, turnings attributed to Symonds Shops, Salem, Massachusetts, 1671–1690; oak. *The Art Institute of Chicago, Sewell L. Avery Fund, Chicago, Illinois.*

13. High Chest of Drawers, New York, 1681–1700; gumwood, tulip, pine, and oak. *The Metropolitan Museum of Art, Rogers Fund, 1936, New York, New York.*

14. Side Chair, Philadelphia, Pennsylvania, or Burlington, New Jersey, 1691–1700; walnut. *The Philadelphia Museum of Art; purchased by subscription and museum funds, Philadelphia, Pennsylvania.*

15. Chest of Drawers, Massachusetts, 1661–1690; oak, pine. *The Shelburne Museum, Shelburne, Vermont.*

16. Armchair, Boston, Massachusetts, 1661–1685; oak, maple. *The Museum of Fine Arts, Boston, Seth K. Sweetster Fund, Boston, Massachusetts.*

17

18

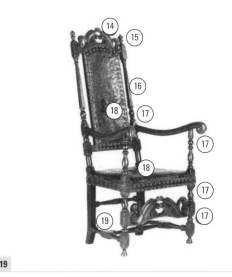

19

20

21

22

William and Mary Style, 1695–1730

1. Spanish, Portuguese, or paintbrush foot
2. Velvet upholstery
3. Horizontally rolled arm
4. Vertically rolled arm support
5. Medial stretcher with double ball-and-ring turnings
6. Loper each side (support hinged lid)
7. Slide for candlestick (each side)
8. Hinged door with fielded panel
9. Cornice
10. Pediment with hood
11. Urn-shaped finial on acroteria (plinth)
12. Double astragal molding
13. Ball-shaped foot
14. Crest with volutes, leaf carving, and C scrolls matches stretcher
15. Finial with ball-over-urn shape
16. Tuscan columnar-turned stile
17. Baluster turning
18. Leather back panel and seat upholstery with brass tacks
19. Stretchers (side, medial, rear)
20. Cavetta molding
21. Cyma reversa molding
22. Flitches of walnut veneer
23. Pendant or drop
24. Stretchers match skirt shape
25. Walnut veneer over facade
26. Star-shaped inlay
27. Herringbone banding
28. Cyma molding
29. Drawer with knob handle
30. Gate-leg (each side) supports hinged leaf
31. Double baluster turning

Taut curves and crisp rectangles create dynamic tension in the style identified with the English monarch William of Orange and his consort Mary. Case furniture is reduced to planes, and the facade often is decorated with boldly grained walnut or maple veneers framed by inlaid bands. Classical moldings are exaggerated in size. Baluster-shaped turnings and C-shaped scrolls create rippling movement. Feet usually are round or oval. An alternate foot—known as "Portuguese," "paintbrush," or "Spanish"—flares into a scroll. Case furniture may be decorated with imitation lacquer known as japanning. It introduces Oriental influence, which continues in the Queen Anne and Chippendale styles (No. 28).

Gate-leg tables and high chests are common forms originating with the Restoration style. High and narrow backs are upholstered, caned, or, in simple furniture, fitted with spindles turned and split in the manner of the Renaissance style. Other forms are daybeds, dressing tables repeating the bases of high chests, side tables, easy chairs, and desks with an occasional upper section fitted as a bookcase. Tea tables and tall case clocks are introduced, but are rare.

The Continental Baroque, with a new emphasis on classicism, determined the style. It was encouraged by the king, his Huguenot designer Daniel Marot, and immigrant Dutch and French craftsmen. They popularize the construction methods of cabinetmakers. Their mortise and tenon joints permit lightweight vertical forms, instead of the horizontal and heavy forms of joiners. Craftsmen in Boston, the largest American city, export furniture to other colonies.

17. Easy Chair, probably Boston, Massachusetts, 1715–1730; maple. *The Museum of Fine Arts, Houston, the Bayou Bend Collection, gift of Miss Ima Hogg, Houston, Texas.*

18. Desk and Bookcase, Boston, Massachusetts, 1701–1735; walnut, white pine. *The Art Institute of Chicago, gift of the Antiquarian Society through the Mr. and Mrs. William Y. Hutchinson Fund, Chicago, Illinois.*

19. Armchair, Boston, Massachusetts, 1695–1710; maple, oak. *The Henry Francis du Pont Winterthur Museum, Winterthur, Delaware.*

20. High Chest of Drawers, New York, 1690–1725; walnut, Southern yellow pine, cedar. *The Art Institute of Chicago, gift of Jamee J. Field and Marshall Field, Chicago, Illinois.*

21. Desk (Scrutoir), probably Boston, Massachusetts, 1690–1720; walnut, white pine. *The Art Institute of Chicago, gift of the Antiquarian Society through Joyce Martin Brown, Lena T. Gilbert, Mrs. Harold T. Martin, and Melinda Martin Vance, Chicago, Illinois.*

22. Table, Massachusetts, 1710–1730; walnut, white pine. *The Art Institute of Chicago, gift of Mr. and Mrs. William Salisbury, Chicago, Illinois.*

① ② ③ ④

23

⑤ ⑥ ⑦ ⑧ ⑨ ⑩ ⑪ ⑫ ⑬ ⑭ ⑮

24

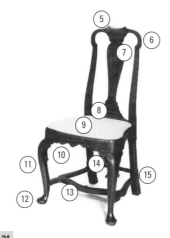

⑯ ⑰ ⑱ ⑲

25

㉕ ㊴ ㊲ ㊳ ㊴ ㉛

26

27

⑳ ㉑ ㉒ ㉓

28

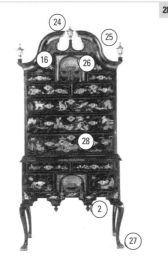

㉔ ㉕ ⑯ ㉖ ㉘ ② ㉗

29

㉔ ㉕ ㉙ ㉚ ㉛ ㉜ ㉝ ㉞ ㉟

㊱

1. Applied molding
2. Pendant
3. Collarino (astragal molding)
4. Pointed slipper foot (mainly Rhode Island and New York)
5. Crest rail with yoke (New England type)
6. Curved shoulder
7. Splat (New England type)
8. Shoe (supports splat)
9. Upholstered compass (shape) slip seat
10. Seat rail with shaped front
11. Cabriole leg
12. Pad foot (mainly New England)
13. Shaped medial and side stretchers (mainly New England)
14. Astragal, or bead, molding
15. Chamfered corners
16. Cyma reversa molding
17. Shaped front and side skirts
18. Knee bracket
19. Disc below turned pad foot
20. Tester
21. Bedstead (wooden framework)
22. Headboard
23. Columnar footposts
24. Scrolled pediment
25. Urn-shaped finial
26. Carved and gilt shell above festoon
27. Lion paw foot (rare)
28. Japanned decoration
29. Inlaid band
30. Mirrored glass panel on hinged door (each side)
31. Pilaster
32. Slide for candlestick
33. Loper each side (support hinged lid)
34. Block front design (mainly New England)
35. Bracket foot (restoration)
36. Winged claw-and-ball foot
37. Face (dial and spandrels)
38. Engaged Corinthian column
39. Roman arch

Curves dominate form. They recur in carved shells on legs, crest rails, and drawers.

Boston and Philadelphia lead in population; styles there differ from Newport and New York City. In New England, chairs include stretchers, and Boston popularizes a convex and concave case form known as "blocking" (No. 29). Front legs on Philadelphia chairs abut seat frame bottoms. Elsewhere, legs continue to the seat rail top and rails abut them at each side. New England favors pad feet and Pennsylvania trifid feet. Slipper feet are occasional in Rhode Island, Connecticut, New York, and Pennsylvania. In the 1740s, claw-and-ball feet refer to the Roman eagle.

Popular forms are gate-leg tables and side chairs. Writing and tea tables appear with circular tilting tops and three legs positioned for room corner storage. Bedsteads with low posts are usual; many occur with high posts; rare ones include cabriole legs with pad feet. Relatively familiar forms are easy chairs, rectangular tea tables, and card tables with a gate leg supporting a hinged top. Rare forms are armchairs, sofas, couches, pier tables, desks and bookcases, chests of drawers, high chests, dressing tables, and tall case clocks.

The style name recognizes evolution in Queen Anne's court (1702–1714), though the style survives to the War of 1812 and even inspires innovative design in the 1980s (No. 156). Oriental influence encourages japanned decoration, usually on a blue-green field (No. 28), and reinforces—if not inspiring—pad feet and cabriole legs. Roman architecture is recalled in moldings, pilasters, columns, and pediments (transformed from a triangle).

Walnut is popular. Cherry, maple, birch, and mahogany are occasional. Figured walnut veneers are rare and mainly in Boston.

23. Tea Table, Newport, Rhode Island, 1740–1760; mahogany. *The Art Institute of Chicago, gift of Sewell L. Avery, Emily Crane Chadbourne, Miss Heath-Jones, Ellen Lamotte, Charles F. Montgomery, Mr. and Mrs. John Trumbull, Russell Tyson, Elizabeth R. Vaughan, and The Wirt D. Walker Fund, Chicago, Illinois.*

24. Side Chair, New England, 1730–1760; walnut. *The Art Institute of Chicago, Robert Allerton Fund, Chicago, Illinois.*

25. Dressing Table, Essex County, Massachusetts, 1750–1770; mahogany, white pine. *The Art Institute of Chicago, gift of the Antiquarian Society through Mrs. William O. Hunt, Jessie Spalding Landon, Mrs. Harold T. Martin, Adelaide Ryerson, and Melinda Martin Vance, Chicago, Illinois.*

26. Tall Clock Case; George Glinn cabinetmaker; Thomas Hughes movement (England); Boston, Massachusetts, 1750 (documented); mahogany with New England white pine. Commissioned by Henry Bromfield (1729–1820) (documented). *The Art Institute of Chicago, Alyce and Edwin DeCosta and Walter E. Heller Foundation, and Harold Stuart Endowments, Chicago, Illinois.*

27. Bedstead, Rhode Island or Massachusetts, 1740–1760; mahogany and maple. *The Henry Francis du Pont Winterthur Museum, Winterthur, Delaware.*

28. High Chest of Drawers; John Pimm, cabinetmaker (signed), japanning possibly by Thomas Johnson, Boston, Massachusetts, 1740–1750; maple, pine. *The Henry Francis du Pont Winterthur Museum, Winterthur, Delaware.*

29. Desk and Bookcase, Richard Walker (attributed), Boston, Massachusetts, 1735–1750; mahogany with oak and white pine secondary woods. *The Art Institute of Chicago, Major Acquisitions Centennial Fund, Chicago, Illinois.*

1. Hinged leaf
2. Applied carved gadrooning
3. *C* Scroll
4. Gate-leg (fifth leg: New York only)
5. Claw-and-ball foot (New York type)
6. Cabriole leg
7. Ogee bracket foot
8. Block-front (New England)
9. Classical wave pattern
10. Loper each side (support hinged lid)
11. Crest rail
12. Splat with lozenge, volutes, and C scrolls
13. Fluted stile
14. Shoe (supports splat)
15. Side rail
16. Front rail with carved applied shell
17. Bracket
18. Acanthus leaf carving
19. Claw-and-ball foot (Philadelphia type)
20. Finial (Philadelphia type)
21. Cornice
22. Applied Rococo carving
23. Face (dial and spandrels)
24. Fluted Doric column
25. Indented fluted quarter-column
26. Scrolled, or broken-arch, pediment
27. Rosette
28. Chamfered and fluted corner
29. Scallop shell
30. Shaped apron or skirt
31. Bombé form
32. Serpentine curve
33. Claw-and-ball foot (Massachusetts type)

Motifs include Chinese frets, Gothic lancet arches and quatrefoils, French rococo serpentine and C-shape scrolls, ribbons, flowers, and leaves, and Roman shells, gadrooning, acanthus leaves, columns, capitals, pilasters, and moldings. The Roman eagle is recalled in claw-and-ball feet varying regionally.

The style adapts London fashion and is named for the English cabinetmaker Thomas Chippendale. His *Gentleman and Cabinet-Makers Director*—a book of furniture designs published in 1754, 1755, and 1762 in London—nourished the style from New York City to Charleston. More influential in Boston is Robert Manwaring's *The Cabinet and Chair-Maker's Real Friend and Companion* (London, 1765).

Mahogany is popular, and walnut, maple, or cherry occasional for Queen Anne forms with diverse ornament. Chests of drawers, clocks, dressing tables often matching high chests, fire screens, tea tables, and looking glasses are fashionable. Easy chairs are frequent. Sofas are rare. Chinese straight legs replace the cabriole late in the period. Ogee bracket feet are popular. A new form is the Pembroke table with straight legs, two drop leaves, and a drawer. Japanning imitates oriental lacquer in New York City and especially Boston (No. 28).

Charleston is a center of craftsmanship with Boston, Newport, New York City, and Philadelphia. New England preferences are chair stretchers and case furniture with concave and convex panels known as "blocking" (Nos. 31, 35). The bombé form is mainly in Boston (No. 36). Rhode Islanders carve distinctive shells and knee designs inspired by acanthus leaves and scrolls elsewhere. Five legs instead of four are on gaming tables in New York City. Philadelphians make the most elaborate furniture in shops with specialists in the London manner. Carved motifs on pediments, skirts, and drawers are pegged and glued in place.

30. Gaming Table, New York, 1755–1790; mahogany, poplar, oak. *The Art Institute of Chicago, gift of Robert Allerton, Bessie Bennett, Mr. and Mrs. Robert Brown, Annie Dunlap Estate, in memory of Annie Wisner, and Mrs. Potter Palmer, Chicago, Illinois.*

31. Desk, probably Norwich, Connecticut, 1755–1805; mahogany, white pine. *The Art Institute of Chicago, gift of the Antiquarian Society through Jessie Spalding Landon, Chicago, Illinois.*

32. Side Chair, Philadelphia, Pennsylvania, 1755–1765; mahogany. *The Art Institute of Chicago, gift of the Robert R. McCormick Charitable Trust, Chicago, Illinois.*

33. Tall Clock Case; John Wood, Jr., movement (Philadelphia); Philadelphia, Pennsylvania, 1765–1775; mahogany with tulipwood. *The Art Institute of Chicago, Helen Bowen Blair Fund, Chicago, Illinois.*

34. High Chest of Drawers, probably Maryland, 1755–1790; mahogany, yellow pine, poplar, cedar. *The Art Institute of Chicago, gift of the Antiquarian Society, Chicago, Illinois.*

35. Bureau Table, John Townsend (attributed), Newport, Rhode Island, 1765–1775; mahogany with maple, chestnut, and white pine. *The Art Institute of Chicago, gift of Jamee J. and Marshall Field, Chicago, Illinois.*

36. Chest of Drawers, John Cogswell (attributed), Boston, Massachusetts, 1783–1795; mahogany, white pine. *The Art Institute of Chicago, the Helen Bowen Blair Fund, Chicago, Illinois.*

37

38

39

40

41

42

1. Shield-shaped back
2. Carved drapery festoon
3. Urn-shaped splat
4. Spade foot
5. Serpentine shape
6. Inlaid flutes
7. Inlaid patera
8. Inlaid husks
9. Serpentine curve
10. Reeding
11. Satinwood veneer
12. Knurling
13. Work bag (access through false drawer)
14. Inlaid urn
15. Stringing (inlaid bands)
16. Castor
17. Urn-shaped finial
18. Muntin
19. Inlaid pilaster
20. Birch veneer
21. Cornice
22. Loper each side (support hinged lid)
23. Hinged top
24. New England foot

Mahogany forms often are veneered, usually with crotch mahogany and panels of maple, birch, or satinwood. Delicate decoration is inlaid, carved, or occasionally painted. Accents are inlaid lines or bands. Straight legs taper in planes or are circular in cross section with reeding. Feet often are bulbous turnings or tapered spades.

Motifs range from Roman bellflowers, paterae, urns, festoons, flutes, acanthus leaves, and pilasters to such contemporary elements as shields, Prince of Wales feathers, or eagles representing both Rome and the new nation. Rococo curves, flowers, and ribbons or Gothic lancet arches and quatrefoils are occasional.

Chippendale forms continue with new delicacy. They include stands, card tables, tall clocks, Pembroke tables, desks, and bookcases. Sofas and chairs occur in great variety. Sideboards and work tables are major new forms, often elaborate.

Large and small cities evolve distinctive variations in form and decoration. Pictorial inlays are imported from England and made in the United States by specialists or craftsmen for personal use. Most New England craftsmen eliminate chair stretchers; craftsmen in Pennsylvania and the South often introduce them.

The style is a simplified version of English neoclassicism. It emphasizes Roman art but includes Greek elements; both are adapted and combined in ways unknown in Classical art. Robert Adam led the movement in English architecture and the decorative arts. He made it popular in the 1760s among fashion leaders, and it reached America slightly during the 1780s to become fashionable in the early 1790s. Influential London pattern books include Alice Hepplewhite's *The Cabinet-Maker and Upholsterer's Guide* (1788; 1789; 1794). Others by Thomas Sheraton are *The Cabinet-Maker and Upholsterer's Drawing-Book* (1791–1794; 1802) and *The Cabinet Dictionary* (1803).

37. Side Chair, carving attributed to Samuel McIntire, Salem, Massachusetts, 1795–1811; mahogany. *The Art Institute of Chicago, gift of the Antiquarian Society through Edith Almy Adams, Chicago, Illinois.*

38. Sideboard, New York City area, 1790–1815; mahogany, white pine, poplar, oak. *The Art Institute of Chicago, gift of the Antiquarian Society through Mrs. Clive Runnells, Chicago, Illinois.*

39. Work Table, Salem, Massachusetts, 1793–1814; mahogany with satinwood and white pine. *The Art Institute of Chicago, gift of the Antiquarian Society through Susan and Richard M. Bennett, Chicago, Illinois.*

40. Pembroke Table, New York City area, 1795–1810; mahogany. *The Art Institute of Chicago, gift of the Illinois District Chapter of the American Institute of Interior Designers and Emily Crane Chadbourne, Chicago, Illinois.*

41. Desk and Bookcase, New Hampshire, 1800–1815; mahogany and birch veneers, white pine. *The Art Institute of Chicago, gift of Mr. and Mrs. Robert Sack, Chicago, Illinois.*

42. Card Table, Royal H. Gould (signed), Chester, Vermont, 1816–1830; cherry with maple veneer. *The Art Institute of Chicago, restricted gift of Mrs. Burton W. Hales, Chicago, Illinois.*

43

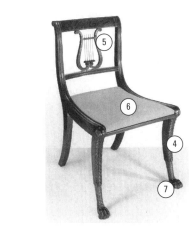

44

45

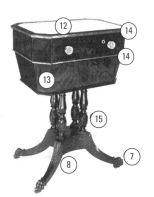

46

47

48

1. Triple elliptic front
2. Back legs rotate when top opened
3. Brass lion foot
4. Leaf carving
5. Lyre-shaped splat
6. Slip seat
7. Carved lion foot
8. Reeding
9. Elliptic front
10. Typical turned shape in New York City
11. Carved dog foot
12. Marble top
13. Canted corner
14. Brass band
15. Whorled baluster
16. Motif of carved reeds tied with bowknot
17. Rosette
18. Serpentine line

No American cabinetmaker is as well known as Duncan Phyfe (1768–1854). His fame was born in his own time, for documents by contemporaries identify their furniture as conforming to Phyfe's style.

Characteristics of it are fine mahogany, excellence in craftsmanship, and restraint in design. Phyfe did not invent the forms or motifs; he adapted them from contemporary English furniture and design books. Significant among his sources is the *London Chair-Maker's and Carver's Book of Prices for Workmanship* first issued in 1802 and reprinted with a supplement in 1808.

Phyfe originally had emigrated from Scotland, where he was trained, to Albany. He was living in New York City by 1792 and developed his firm with the extraordinary growth of the city. He eventually managed perhaps 40 employees, in contrast to most contemporary firms with less than 12, and probably 3–6, workers. Phyfe not only dominated the craft in his adopted city, but he also sold furniture in the coastal trade to the South. As his firm developed, Phyfe became more of an executive than a craftsman.

Very little furniture can be securely identified with Phyfe's shop through labels, bills, or histories of ownership. Attributions cannot at present be made on the basis of carved motifs, general designs, or construction because employees often moved between shops, and owners subcontracted work among themselves and to such specialists as carvers and turners.

Phyfe's style is an enduring one. Craftsmen revived it and even forged it with the concern for antique furniture in the late nineteenth century. Manufacturers have continued this style through the twentieth century. Later in his career Phyfe adopted other styles (Nos. 66, 67), which are not identified with his name.

43. Card Table, Phyfe style, New York City, 1810–1820; mahogany. *The Henry Francis du Pont Winterthur Museum, Winterthur, Delaware.*

44. Side Chair, Phyfe style, New York City, 1810–1820; mahogany. *The Henry Francis du Pont Winterthur Museum, Winterthur, Delaware.*

45. Chest of Drawers, Phyfe style, New York City, 1810–1820; mahogany, tulip, and white pine. *The Henry Francis du Pont Winterthur Museum, Winterthur, Delaware.*

46. Work Table, Duncan Phyfe Shop (label), New York City, 1815–1816; mahogany, tulip, white pine. *The Henry Francis du Pont Winterthur Museum, Winterthur, Delaware.*

47. Sofa, Michael Allison Shop (stamp), New York City, circa 1814–circa 1817; mahogany with maple. *The Art Institute of Chicago, Gift of the Antiquarian Society in honor of Milo M. Naeve, Chicago, Illinois.*

48. Armchair, Duncan Phyfe Shop (documented), New York City, 1807; mahogany. *The Henry Francis du Pont Winterthur Museum, Winterthur, Delaware.*

49

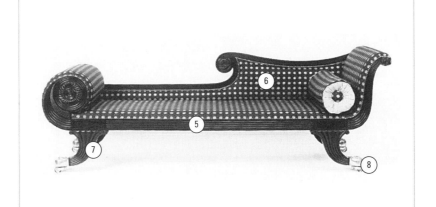

50

51

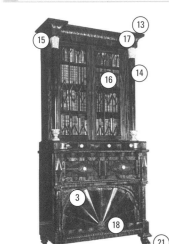

52

53

54

55

The Classical world is revived with Grecian emphasis and Egyptian or Gothic accent. "Grecian" often is synonymous with "Classical," because limited information about the isolated region leads to confusion between Classical arts.

Lion feet and couches are among motifs and forms interpreted with the greatest accuracy since Roman art gained new vitality in the 15th century Italian Renaissance. Forms and motifs originally in bronze or marble are in wood.

Form and carving in the period are increasingly bold and simplified. New York City is the fashion center and remains so through the century. Variations evolve in Boston, Philadelphia, and Baltimore.

London pattern books relevant to America are cabinet-makers' handbooks, Thomas Hope's *Household Furniture* of 1807, George Smith's echo of it entitled *Household Furniture and Interior Decoration* in 1808, Rudolph Ackermann's periodical entitled the *Repository of the Arts* from 1809 to 1829, and Thomas King's books, especially *The Modern Style of Cabinet Work Exemplified* published in 1829.

The *Klismos* chair is a major form (No. 49). The French introduce adaptations from ancient Greek vases and sculpture in the early 1790s, the English about 1800, and Americans about 1802. The form is usual by 1810 and popular in many styles into the 1840s (Nos. 51, 63). Early examples are the most accurate in form.

Diverse designs reveal English influence. Furniture moved from walls into rooms requires appealing design from every view. Aside from chairs, popular seating forms are stools (often in Roman curule form), window seats, and sofas (also known as settees). Sideboards are usual. Tall clocks drift from fashion. Marble is popular for table tops and occasionally columnar legs. Feet, moldings, and table supports in New York City may be gilt, and stencil gilt designs simulate ormolu. The usual wood is mahogany. Rosewood is occasional. Veneers in mahogany are common.

49. Side Chair, Benjamin Henry Latrobe, designer; Thomas Wetherill, maker; George Bridport, decorator (documented); Philadelphia, Pennsylvania; circa 1808; yellow poplar, oak, maple, and white pine. *The Museum of Fine Arts, Houston, The Bayou Bend Collection, Agnes Cullen Arnold Endowment Fund, Houston, Texas.*

50. Grecian Couch, New England, 1810–1835; mahogany, birch, and white pine. *The Art Institute of Chicago, gift of Joseph P. Antonow, Chicago, Illinois.*

51. Side Chair, Sherlock Spooner and George Trask (stamp), Boston, Massachusetts, 1825–1826; mahogany with white pine slip seat frame. *The Art Institute of Chicago, restricted gift of Mrs. Harold T. Martin, Chicago, Illinois.*

52. Desk and Bookcase, Antoine Gabriel Quervelle (label), Philadelphia, Pennsylvania, circa 1835; mahogany with poplar. *The Munson-Williams-Proctor Institute, Utica, New York.*

53. Sideboard with Knife Boxes, attributed to Joseph B. Barry, Philadelphia, Pennsylvania, 1810–1822; mahogany, mahogany veneer, poplar. *The Henry Francis du Pont Winterthur Museum, Winterthur, Delaware.*

54. Fire-screen, probably New York City, 1810–1820, mahogany. *The Henry Francis du Pont Winterthur Museum, Winterthur, Delaware.*

55. Center Table, New York City, 1821–1835; rosewood veneer and oak. Credible tradition of commission by Stephen Whitney. *The Museum of the City of New York, Gift of Mrs. Egerton L. Winthrop, New York, New York.*

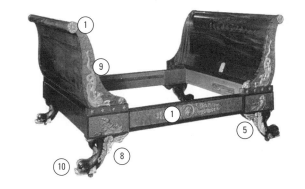

56

57

58

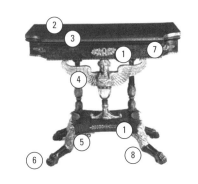

59

60

61

62

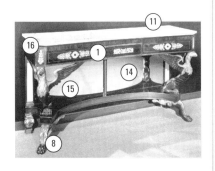

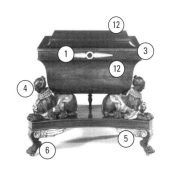

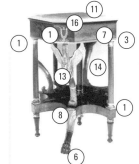

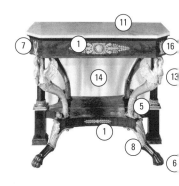

Empire Style, 1810–1820

Winged female busts, swans, dolphins, and other motifs revive Roman art. They are on forms made or veneered in polished mahogany and occasionally rosewood. Satinwood panels and ormolu accent surfaces. Carved elements often are painted green, suggesting bronze patina, or gilt. The style is rare because it was expensive in materials and labor.

The French style refers to Napoleon Bonaparte's empire from 1804 to 1815. Evolution before his reign gained momentum as the architects Charles Percier and Pierre F. L. Fontaine met his order for refurnishing official buildings stripped during the revolution. Their results appeared in the 1801 and 1812 editions of *Recuil de decorations intérieures*. Among simplifiers of the official style, Pierre de la Mésangère published designs from 1802 to 1835 in the *Collection des meubles et objets de goût* of Paris and Rudolph Ackermann from 1809 to 1828 in the *Repository of Arts* in London. The style reached the United States through these publications, American travelers, and French furniture and craftsmen.

Charles-Honoré Lannuier (1779–1819) was significant among them, judging by his furniture. The Parisian immigrated to New York City, the American center of the style, about 1803 and was active there and in coastal trade. Others participated in the style. Eagle and wing supports are even cited in the *New-York Book of Prices for Manufacturing Cabinet and Chair Work* in 1817.

New forms are secretaries with facades lowering as writing surfaces, small circular tables, corner stands, and bedsteads parallel to walls below half-circular curtain frames. Sideboards are an accommodation to English forms (No. 59).

56. Card Table, Charles-Honoré Lannuier Shop (label), New York City, 1817; mahogany, mahogany veneer, basswood, ash, cherry, eastern white pine, and yellow-poplar. Commissioned by William Bayard, probably for Maria and Duncan Parsall Campbell. *The Albany Institute of History and Art, gift of Stephen van Rensselaer Crosby, Albany.*

57. Bedstead, Charles-Honoré Lannuier Shop (label), New York City, 1817–1819; mahogany, elm, ash, eastern white pine, maple, cherry, and rosewood veneer. Commissioned by Stephen van Rensselaer IV (1789–1868). *The Albany Institute of History and Art, gift of Constance van Rensselaer Thayer Dexter, Albany, New York.*

58. Pier Table, Charles-Honoré Lannuier Shop (label), New York City, 1817; mahogany, mahogany veneer, eastern white pine, maple, and yellow-poplar. Commissioned by William Bayard, probably for Maria and Duncan Parsall Campbell. *The Albany Institute of History and Art, gift of Stephen van Rensselaer Crosby, Albany, New York.*

59. Sideboard, New York City, 1810–1820; rosewood with ebony. *The Los Angeles County Museum of Art, Museum Acquisition Fund, Los Angeles, California.*

60. Cellerette, New York City, 1810–1820; mahogany, rosewood veneer, eastern white pine, maple, ebony, and yellow-poplar. Credible tradition of commission by Stephen Ball Munn (1766–1855). *Yale University Art Gallery, Mabel Brady Garvan Collection, New Haven, Connecticut.*

61. Corner Table, Charles-Honoré Lannuier Shop (label), New York City, 1817 and circa 1840; mahogany, mahogany veneer, eastern white pine, and maple. Commissioned by William Bayard, probably for Maria and Duncan Parsall Campbell. *The Albany Institute of History and Art, Gift of Justine van Rensselaer Barber Hooper, Albany, New York.*

62. Piano, James Stewart (stamp), Baltimore, 1818; mahogany. *The Art Institute of Chicago, gift of Mrs. Herbert P. McLaughlin, Chicago.*

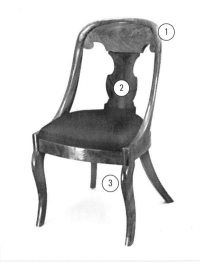

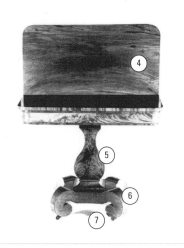

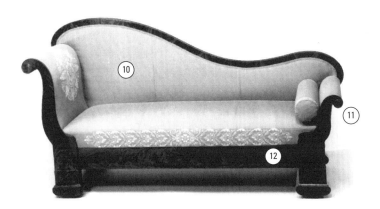

63

64

65

66

6

French Restauration Style, 1830–1850

Simplicity, practicality, and comfort mark the French Restauration style. Born in France, it evolved during restoration of the Bourbons to the throne, from 1814 to 1848. Undulating curves balance geometric forms. Plain surfaces are relieved by spare ornament. The style includes the Egyptian lotus, circles, ormolu, and such simple moldings as the astragal. White marble and particularly the rich color and grain of mahogany veneers are significant to this style.

Forms often are conservative versions of the late Empire style. Card tables retain the single pedestal, sofas an asymmetrical shape, and stools the curule form. Chairs are inspired by the *klismos* shape in classical Greece, but they typically are transformed by curves in the crest, urn-shaped splats, braces curved from crest to seat, and the shape of legs.

Simplicity of the French Restauration style encouraged interpretations over a long period in large and small centers of craftsmanship from Boston to New Orleans. Pierre de la Mésangère's Parisian periodical *Collection de meubles et objects de goût* recorded the style in France; George Smith's *Cabinet-Maker and Upholsterer's Guide,* published in 1826 in London, offered the English variation; John Hall's *The Cabinet Maker's Assistant,* published in 1840 in Baltimore, recorded a version in the United States.

63. Side Chair *(Chaise Gondole),* probably New York City, 1835–1850; mahogany. *The Museum of Fine Arts, Houston, the Bayou Bend Collection, gift of Miss Ima Hogg, Houston, Texas.*

64. Card Table, New York City, 1836–1845; mahogany. *The New-York Historical Society, New York, New York.*

65. Library Chair, probably New York City, 1831–1840; mahogany. *Historic Hudson Valley, Sunnyside, Tarrytown, New York.*

66. Daybed *(Méridienne),* attributed to Duncan Phyfe (documented), New York City, 1837; mahogany. *The Metropolitan Museum of Art, purchase, L. E. Katzenbach Foundation gift, 1966, New York, New York.*

67. Pier Table, attributed to Duncan Phyfe (documented), New York City, 1831–1840; mahogany with marble top. *The Metropolitan Museum of Art, purchase, Edgar J. Kaufmann, Jr., Foundation Fund, 1968, New York, New York.*

68

69

70

71

72

7,

1. Machine banding
2. Octagonal column
3. Wheel-shaped back
4. Crocket
5. Trefoil
6. Finial
7. Trefoil arch
8. Quatrefoil
9. Pendant or drop
10. Ogee arch
11. Roman arch
12. Cluster column
13. Maple veneer
14. Plinth
15. Lancet arch
16. Mirror
17. Marble
18. Castor

Pointed arches, trefoils, quatrefoils, tracery, crockets, Tudor roses, and clustered columns from the architectural style common in western Europe between the twelfth and sixteenth centuries are adapted to the mid-nineteenth-century furniture forms. Among them the étagère, or what-not, and dining tables extended by mechanical parts are newly popular.

Medieval furniture forms are not reproduced. They were generally unrecognized in a period of vague historical knowledge, and those known did not meet the comforts and needs of contemporary life.

Walnut and oak are common woods. Mahogany and rosewood are occasional. Silhouettes are bold; carved details accent plain surfaces.

English fashion inspired the Gothic Revival style. It never gained the popularity it held abroad, but the motifs had been a consistent theme since the mid-eighteenth-century Chippendale Style.

Contemporaries also knew the Gothic Revival style as *Medieval*. Significant books offering designs are A. W. Pugin's *Gothic Furniture in the Style of the Fifteenth Century*, published in London in 1835, and Robert Conner's *Cabinet Maker's Assistant*, published in New York City in 1842.

68. Extension Dining Table, New York City, 1842–1845; mahogany. *The Munson-Williams-Proctor Institute, gift of Mrs. Erving Pruyn, Utica, New York.*

69. Side Chair, designed by Alexander Jackson Davis (documented), probably 1841, made by Richard Byrne, Dobbs Ferry, New York, or Ambrose Wright, Hastings (now Hastings-on-Hudson), New York, circa 1842; oak. *Lyndhurst, a property of the National Trust for Historic Preservation, Tarrytown, New York.*

70. Armchair, New York City, 1841–1850; oak. *The Art Institute of Chicago, restricted gift of Jeffrey Shedd, Chicago, Illinois.*

71. Chest of drawers and mirror, United States, circa 1846–1866; walnut, maple. *The Smithsonian Institution, the National Museum of History and Technology, Washington, D.C., gift of the city of Bridgeport, Connecticut.*

72. Étagère, probably New York City, 1845–1855; rosewood with marble top. *The Brooklyn Museum, H. Randolph Lever Fund, New York, New York.*

73. Settee, Thomas Brooks (attributed), Brooklyn, New York, circa 1846; walnut, cherry. *The Society for the Preservation of New England Antiquities, Boston: Bowen House, Woodstock, Connecticut, Gift of Margaret Carson Holt (Photograph by Richard Cheek), Boston, Massachusetts.*

74

75

76

77

78

Ball and spiral turnings, strapwork, and flowers with leaves are features of the Elizabethan style. Less popular in America than in England, it is mainly confined in the United States to chairs in walnut, mahogany, or rosewood, and to informal painted bedroom suites known as "cottage furniture."

The period of greatest popularity was at mid-century. Vague historical knowledge wrongly credited many motifs and chairs with high backs to the reign of Queen Elizabeth, instead of correctly assigning them to the Restoration and the William and Mary styles of England.

The Elizabethan style frequently mingled with the contemporary Rococo Revival and other styles. It is a variant of the Renaissance Revival style, based on English and French sources. The style lingered through the late nineteenth and early twentieth centuries as an accent for rooms furnished in other styles.

Walter Scott's novels during the 1820s influenced concern for the "Elizabethan" period, as did Henry Shaw's investigation of English antique furniture titled *Specimens of Ancient Furniture,* published in London in 1836. Robert Bridgen's influential designs for this style appeared in his *Furniture with Candelabra and Interior Decoration,* published in London in 1838.

74. Side Chair, Herter Brothers (documented), New York City, circa 1869; rosewood. From LeGrand Lockwood house, Norwalk, Connecticut. *The Art Institute of Chicago, Wesley M. Dixon, Jr. Fund, Chicago, Illinois.*

75. Chest of Drawers and Mirror, probably New York City, circa 1850; painted pine. *Historic Hudson Valley, Sunnyside, Tarrytown, New York.*

76. Side Chair, probably New York City, circa 1851–1861; rosewood, mahogany. *The Museum of the City of New York, gift of Mrs. Henry De Bevoise Schenck, New York, New York.*

77. Armchair, Merklen Brothers (attributed), New York City, circa 1885; mahogany. *The Brooklyn Museum of Art, Gift of Miss Eleanor Curnow in Memory of her Mother, Mary Griffith Curnow, New York, New York.*

78. Armchair, United States, 1850–1860; mahogany. *Harriet Beecher Stowe Center, Hartford, Connecticut.*

79

80

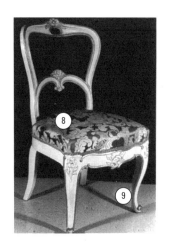

81

82

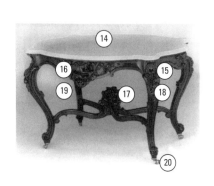

83

84

85

1. Mirror
2. Rose flower and leaves
3. Cabriole leg
4. Acanthus leaf
5. Cartouche
6. S scroll
7. C scroll
8. Silk damask upholstery
9. Scroll foot
10. Finial
11. Console
12. Serpentine curve (laminated wood)
13. Scallop shell
14. Marble top
15. Shell motif
16. Apron or skirt
17. Basket of flowers
18. Fruit motif
19. Carved hound chasing fox (opposite side)
20. Castor
21. Saltire stretcher

Curves in serpentine or C shapes are the basis for furniture form. They mingle in decoration with scallop shells, leaves, flowers—especially the rose—baskets of flowers, the acanthus, and the cabochon. Legs are cabriole in form and often terminate in scroll feet. Contemporaries knew this style as the *Louis Quatorze,* the *Louis Quinze,* or the *Antique French.* It is favored for bedrooms and parlors.

Rococo taste in the court of Louis XV was the main precedent. Craftsmen made some reproductions, but inaccurate knowledge of historic styles and an eclectic approach to designing led to form and decoration revived from French furniture of the late-seventeenth century to the mid-eighteenth. Motifs are combined and boldly reinterpreted from original delicacy. Side tables, sofas, chairs, and other eighteenth-century forms are extended with "tête-à-tête" chairs with curved backs, and the étagère, or whatnot, for displaying objects.

Sources dictated walnut and painted woods. But rosewood and mahogany are usual in the revival. Woods are laminated, as in the Naturalistic style, for achieving strength for delicate designs. Cast iron briefly appears in sophisticated furniture (No. 84).

The revival emerged in England and France during the 1820s, became a movement by the 1840s, and reigned in America during the 1850s. Designers often combined the cabriole leg and motifs with the Naturalistic style. Features survive in mass-produced furniture into the 1880s.

The style reached America through many sources. They include contemporary imported French furniture and immigrant craftsmen, such as the German John Henry Belter.

Furniture in international trade exhibitions and illustrations in periodicals support popularity. Significant are books and periodicals by the Parisian Desiré Guilmard, especially his *Le Garde-meuble, ancien et moderne, journal d'ameublement.* It begins reporting French fashions in 1839 and continues through many styles until 1935.

79. Étagère, New York City, 1850–1870; rosewood with laminated woods and marble top. *The Art Institute of Chicago, Elizabeth R. Vaughan Fund, Chicago, Illinois.*

80. Pier Mirror, United States, circa 1853; gilt wood. *The Metropolitan Museum of Art, gift of Mrs. Frederick Wildman, 1964, New York, New York.*

81. Side Chair, New York City, 1845–1855; painted and gilt mahogany. *The New York State Museum, Albany, New York.*

82. Étagère, New York City, 1850–1860; rosewood with marble top. *The Newark Museum, Newark, New Jersey, gift of the Museum of the City of New York, 1934.*

83. Center Table, Doe, Hazelton and Company (label), Boston, Massachusetts, 1847–1857; mahogany and marble. *The Art Institute of Chicago, gift of Brooks and Hope B. McCormick, Chicago, Illinois.*

84. Center Table, Walter Bryent designer for Chase Brothers and Company (label), Boston, Massachusetts, 1852; cast iron painted to simulate rosewood. *The Art Institute of Chicago, Wesley M. Dixon, Jr., Fund, Chicago, Illinois.*

85. Library Table, John Henry Belter Firm (label), 1851–1861; rosewood. *The Art Institute of Chicago, gift of Gloria and Richard Manney, Chicago, Illinois.*

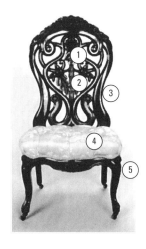

86

87

88

89

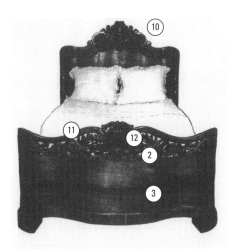

Naturalistic Style, 1850–1865

Fruit and flowers as well as leaves of the grape, oak, or rose are prominent in the Naturalistic style. Carving is realistic, in contrast to generalization in the eighteenth century.

The style frequently merges with the contemporary Rococo Revival style. Forms are identical and scrolls in serpentine and C shapes, scallop shells, and the cabochon mingle with the motifs from nature.

Designs often are accomplished with a lamination process. Though a European construction, it reached a new level of American sophistication in the firm founded by the German immigrant John Henry Belter. Several layers of wood, each one-sixteenth of an inch thick, are glued together with the grain at right angles. Layers vary from three to sixteen, the average being six to eight. Panels are steamed in molds for undulating forms of such strength that a tracery of motifs could be carved into the backs of sofas and chairs or the skirts of tables. Superimposed carved elements increase the three-dimensional effect. Mahogany, walnut, and rosewood are favored as surface woods.

The style evolved with the English Rococo Revival during the 1820s. It parallels movements in English painting, sculpture, or silver, and their echoes in the American arts. Advances in botany and the invention of photography support patronage for realism. In furniture, the style assumes an original character in the United States through intricate carving permitted by the lamination process.

86. Side Chair, John Henry Belter Firm (attributed), New York City, 1850–1867; rosewood with laminated woods. *The Art Institute of Chicago, gift of Gloria and Richard Manney, Chicago, Illinois.*

87. Center Table, John Henry Belter Firm (label), New York City, 1856–1861; rosewood with laminated woods and marble top. *The Museum of the City of New York, gift of Mr. and Mrs. Gunther Vieter, New York, New York.*

88. Bedstead, John Henry Belter Firm (label), New York City, 1850–1860; rosewood with laminated woods. *The Brooklyn Museum of Art, gift of Mrs. Ernest Vietor, New York, New York.*

89. Sofa, John Henry Belter Firm (attributed), New York City, circa 1856; rosewood with laminated woods. *The Victoria and Albert Museum, London, England.*

90

91

92

93

94

1. Ormolu
2. Silk damask upholstery
3. Castor
4. Hinged leaf
5. Floral and ribbon carving
6. Tapered and fluted leg
7. Classical egg-and-dart motif
8. Ebonized maple
9. Ceramic plaque with ormolu frame
10. Incised gilt decoration
11. Marquetry
12. Porcelain plaque with ormolu frame
13. Amboina veneer
14. Ivory inlay
15. Ionic column with ormolu
16. Medial stretcher with urn

Rectangular shapes are contrasted with ovals and arches, straight and tapered legs are fluted, and plain surfaces are accented with classical moldings, columns, wreaths, garlands, urns, lyres, acanthus, and beading. The Louis XVI style is one of the few revivals in the mid-nineteenth century of an earlier period in form as well as decoration. But the revival is identified by bolder design and differences in craftsmanship and woods than in the monarch's reign from 1754 to 1793.

The long period of popularity includes many variations. They range from an initial period of exaggerated motifs in the 1850s and their close imitation in the 1860s to novel adaptations through the period. The style flourished in New York City. There it was a specialty among French decorators, usually with their own shops for making furniture.

Costly materials and elaborate workmanship are characteristic. Rosewood or ebonized woods are favored in the earliest versions though the woods were not used in the eighteenth century. Walnut occurs with the 1890s. Dark woods contrast with gilt metal mounts, elaborate marquetry, panels of light woods, ivory inlays, and porcelain plaques. These decorative elements usually were imported from Paris, where several firms kept a branch. Carving is featured during the 1850s.

The English and the French originated this style. Eugenie, consort to Napoleon III, endorsed and popularized it after 1853, when it became known by the alternate name of the "Marie Antoinette" Style. The straight leg and motifs are often adapted to forms of Renaissance Revival and Neo-Greek styles.

90. Armchair, Leon Marcotte and Co. (attributed), New York City, circa 1860; ebonized cherry and gilt metal mounts. *The Art Institute of Chicago, restricted gift of Marilyn and Thomas L. Karsten in honor of her parents, Gertrude and Perry S. Herst, Chicago, Illinois.*

91. Card Table, Alexander Roux (label), New York City, 1850–1857; rosewood. *The Brooklyn Museum of Art, H. Randolph Lever Fund, New York, New York.*

92. Cabinet (one of a pair), Leon Marcotte and Co. (attributed), New York City, circa 1860; ebonized maple with ormolu, ceramic plaque, and gilt moldings. *The Metropolitan Museum of Art, gift of Mrs. Chester D. Noyes, 1968, New York, New York.*

93. Cabinet, Alexander Roux (label), New York City, 1866 (documented); rosewood with porcelain plaques and gilt mounts. *The Metropolitan Museum of Art, Edgar J. Kaufmann, Jr., Charitable Foundation Fund, 1968, New York, New York.*

94. Library Table, Leon Marcotte and Co. (attributed), New York City, circa 1872; walnut, mahogany, pine, and amboina with hornbeam, ivory inlay, and gilt metal mounts. *The Metropolitan Museum of Art, gift of Mrs. Robert W. de Forest, 1934, New York, New York.*

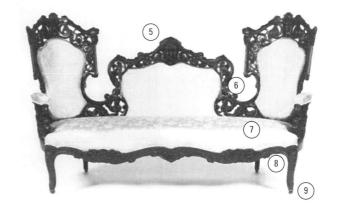

Renaissance Revival Style, 1851–1880

Renaissance, Baroque, and Mannerist approaches to design, especially in sixteenth- and seventeenth-century France, are combined in a period of vague historical knowledge to inspire the bold Renaissance Revival style enduring through freedom of interpretation. Variations range form florid and curvilinear during the 1850s to severe and angular by the 1870s (see No. 118). Form enters the revival in the 1890s and survives to the 1920s. The Elizabethan style is a variant based on English rather than French and Italian sources.

Common motifs are flowers, fruit, game, classical busts, bizarre faces known as "masks," acanthus scrolls, strapwork, and tassels. They are carved in high relief, and many recur in imported porcelain or marquetry insets on case furniture and table tops. Significant architectural motifs adapted to furniture are pediments, pilasters, columns, balusters, brackets, and volutes.

This style often merges in form and decoration with others. Cabriole legs and other elements of the Rococo Revival appear in the 1850s. They tend to disappear in the 1860s before straight legs and motifs from the Louis XVI style or the cloven hoof associated with it and the Egyptian Revival.

Mahogany and walnut are favored woods. Rosewood and ebony are occasional. Burled walnut panels are featured by the 1870s. Upholstery, especially in chairs, is prominent.

95. Armchair, John Jelliff (attributed), Newark, New Jersey, 1860–1870; rosewood. *The Newark Museum, gift of Mrs. John Laimbeer, Jr., 1936, Newark, New Jersey.*

96. Sofa, Charles A. Baudouine Firm (attributed), New York City, 1849–1854; laminated mahogany. *The Art Institute of Chicago, gift of Mr. and Mrs. Louis J. Fischer, Chicago, Illinois.*

97. Étagère, Julius Dessoir (label), New York City, 1855–1865; rosewood. *The Metropolitan Museum of Art, purchase, Edgar J. Kaufmann Jr. Foundation Gift, 1969, New York, New York.*

98. Piano, Robert Nunns and John Clark Firm (label), New York City, 1851 (documented); rosewood. *The Metropolitan Museum of Art, gift of George Lowther, 1906, New York, New York.*

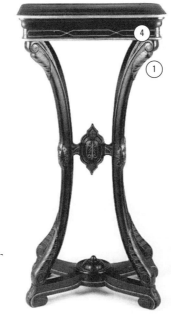

1. Anthemion
2. Greek curule shape
3. Hoof foot
4. Incised gilt lines
5. Boss
6. Fluted pilaster
7. Lion head
8. Medial stretcher
9. Castor
10. Finial
11. Burl walnut panel
12. Greek key design
13. Metal plaque
14. Plinth

Curved and rectangular elements boldly contrast in shapes. Common motifs from ancient Greek architecture and ornaments are pilasters, columns, flutes, acroteria, foliate scrolls, anthemia, and the Greek key design. They are carved in high relief, inlaid in contrasting light and dark woods, or incised and gilded.

The alternate names of "New" and "Modern" Greek identify a different interpretation of sources than in the earlier Classical style. Motifs are exaggerated in size, changed in proportion, and combined in new ways. Taut curves and crisp angles are tensely balanced. The shapes of the Greek curule and *klismos* chairs are revived. Feet vary from the cloven hoof to scrolls. Case furniture often rests on a high plinth.

The French originated the Neo-Greek style, and the English quickly adopted it. The style reached the United States in the late 1850s, became popular in the 1860s, and influenced factory furniture into the 1880s. Motifs often merge with the contemporary Louis XVI and Renaissance Revival styles.

99. Stool, Alexander Roux (label), New York City, circa 1865; painted woods. *The Metropolitan Museum of Art, purchase, Edgar J. Kaufmann, Jr. Charitable Foundation Fund, 1969, New York, New York.*

100. Stand, New York City, circa 1870; ebonized cherry. *The Metropolitan Museum of Art, purchase, Edgar J. Kaufmann, Jr. Foundation Gift, 1968, New York, New York.*

101. Armchair, New York City, 1860–1870; ebonized walnut. *The Brooklyn Museum of Art, gift of Sarah Fanning Chapman and Bertha Fanning Taylor, New York, New York.*

102. Bedstead, Nelson, Matter, and Company, Grand Rapids, Michigan, 1870–1880; walnut. *The Margaret Woodbury Strong Museum, gift of Mr. and Mrs. John C. Doolittle, Rochester, New York.*

103. Music Cabinet, George Croome (label), Boston, Massachusetts, 1875–1877; mahogany, rosewood. *The Art Institute of Chicago, Elizabeth R. Vaughan Fund, Chicago, Illinois.*

104

105

106

107

Egyptian Revival Style, 1865–1890

1. Gilt bronze head
2. Original tapestry upholstery
3. Gilt incised ornament
4. Claw-and-ball foot
5. Castor
6. Egyptian stool form
7. Lotus capital
8. Cluster column
9. Marble top
10. Winged orb
11. Lion paw foot
12. Medial stretcher

Egyptian heads, clustered columns, lotus capitals, winged orbs, zigzag lines, palmettes, the cloven hoof, and paw-shaped feet are Egyptian motifs emerging as occasional motifs early in the nineteenth century and combined with others late in the century for the Egyptian Revival style. Popularity is limited.

Tables, chairs, stands, and stools mainly are common forms of the late nineteenth century with motifs adapted to them. The Egyptian stool with a concave seat and turned stretchers and legs is the principal revival of an ancient form.

Treatment of motifs may show contrasting elements, even on a single piece of furniture, from shallow relief to three-dimensional exuberance. Gilt decoration is common against dark and often ebonized woods. Exotic combinations of materials include woods, marble, and gilt bronze.

English fashion encouraged the Egyptian style. Monuments or artifacts in tombs from about 2700 B.C. to about 1000 B.C. are the main source for motifs. Exhibition of Egyptian antiquities in the international exposition at London in 1862, completion of the Suez Canal in 1869, and British concern with Egyptian affairs after 1876 all stimulated interest in Egypt and Egyptian art.

104. Armchair, Auguste Pottier and William P. Stymus (attributed), New York City, 1870–1880; rosewood, gilt metal. *The Art Institute of Chicago, restricted gift of Suzanne Waller Worthy, Chicago, Illinois.*

105. Stool, United States, 1870–1880; oak. *The Newark Museum, bequest of Susan Dwight Bliss, 1967, Newark, New Jersey.*

106. Stool, United States, 1870–1880; maple painted black. *The Metropolitan Museum of Art, Rogers Fund, 1967, New York, New York.*

107. Center Table, Auguste Pottier and William P. Stymus (attributed), New York City, 1870–1880; rosewood, marble. *The Metropolitan Museum of Art, anonymous gift, 1968, New York, New York.*

108

109

110

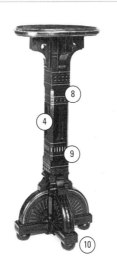

111

112

113

114

1. White enamel paint
2. Leather upholstery
3. Stylized flower
4. Chamfer
5. Triangle motif
6. Bracket
7. Grooves
8. Incised lines
9. Geometric ornament
10. Ball foot
11. Crocket
12. Roman arch
13. Fielded panel
14. Spindles
15. Stylized leaves
16. Sunflowers and leaves
17. Finial
18. Flying buttress (Gothic architectural adaptation)
19. Cornice

English efforts for reforming clumsy form, decoration, and construction in furniture reached Americans in the 1870s. Formal training of English designers began as early as 1835 for improving quality to compete with Europe. Reform gained a visual program with an intellectual basis in Augustus Welby Pugin's *True Principles of Pointed and Christian Architecture* of 1841. He writes that furniture, as well as buildings, should be designed with ornament secondary to form and that form should evolve from function. Both were a reaction to the Gothic Style in furniture: Regency forms with Gothic architectural decoration.

Disappointment over English manufactures in the Great Exhibition of 1851 further encouraged change. Architects advance the cause by designing furniture for Reform buildings. Americans continue their ambitious adaptation of Gothic architecture to massive sideboards, even to flying buttresses of Roman arches visually implying support (Nos. 113, 114). The principle of obvious structure continues in other forms (No. 110).

Charles Locke Eastlake popularizes furniture reform in *Hints on Household Taste,* published in London in 1868. Americans bought nine editions from 1872 to 1890. Eastlake follows reform principles by relating form, function, and craftsmanship, approves carving or inlay by hand and condemns machine imitations of them. Eastlake differs from his contemporaries by seeking design principles in every period, as well as the Gothic. He was chagrined that his approach of simple decoration by grooves, chamfers, geometric ornament, and spindles led to manufactured furniture named for him in the late 1870s. But he would have been encouraged by the breakfast suite Louis Comfort Tiffany commissioned in 1885 after experimenting with function and design principles in American furniture since 1882 (Nos. 108, 109).

American furniture in the Reform style is rare. But Reform principles continue in Art Furniture styles, Arts and Crafts styles, and International styles.

108. Armchair, Louis Comfort Tiffany, designer, made by Barnes Brothers as subcontractors for Ernest Hagen and J. Matthew Meier Shop (documented), New York City, 1885, maple painted white with brown leather upholstery. From the Tiffany House, Madison Avenue at 72nd Street, New York City. *The Art Institute of Chicago, anonymous gift, Chicago, Illinois.*

109. Breakfast Table, Louis Comfort Tiffany, designer for Ernest Hagen and J. Matthew Meier Shop (documented), New York City, 1885; pine painted white. From the Tiffany House, Madison Avenue at 72nd Street, New York City. *The Art Institute of Chicago, anonymous gift, Chicago, Illinois.*

110. Armchair, New York City, circa 1876; maple. *Sagamore Hill National Historic Site, National Park Service, Oyster Bay, New York.*

111. Bookcase, William Homes Company (label), Boston, Massachusetts, circa 1876; oak. *The Hudson River Museum, gift of the Doran family, Yonkers, New York.*

112. Pedestal, New York City, 1870–1880; ebonized cherry. *The Metropolitan Museum of Art, purchase, Edgar J. Kaufmann, Jr. Charitable Foundation Gift, 1969, New York, New York.*

113. Sideboard, Herter Brothers (incised stamp), New York City, 1870–1876; oak, white pine. *The Art Institute of Chicago, Robert R. McCormick Charitable Trust, Chicago, Illinois.*

114. Bookcase, Isaac E. Scott (documented), Chicago, Illinois, 1875; walnut. *The Chicago Architecture Foundation, Chicago, Illinois.*

115

116

117

118

119

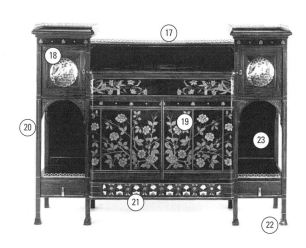

120

"Art" is vaguely linked to "furniture" during the 1870s for identifying an English fashion. Charles Locke Eastlake used the term in *Hints on Household Taste,* published in London in 1868 and in the United States in nine editions from 1872 to 1890. He probably coined the term, though the English reformer Thomas Cole used "Art Manufactures" as early as 1847. Eastlake's purpose was separating manufactured furniture from that of the Reform style. His term is common among innovative Americans during the 1870s and was commercialized from the late 1870s into the 1890s.

Not a precise term historically, today it generally separates the intellectualized and massive Reform style from its exotic and delicate strand. The furniture usually is costly in materials and workmanship. The crest of the movement is in New York City from the mid-1870s to the mid-1880s with Herter Brothers preeminent in the style. It lingers there and elsewhere to World War I.

Forms vary from eclectic to original. Tall clocks, inspired by eighteenth-century examples, return to favor. Historic forms also are adapted to new uses in England and repeated in America, such as court cupboards of the Renaissance style for chests of drawers (compare Nos. 9 and 118). Even a Reform movement chair by E. W. Godwin in 1869 is transformed in England and America into luxurious delicacy (No. 116). A leading catalogue and guide to the movement is the London publication of 1877 entitled *Art Furniture Designed by Edward W. Godwin F.S.A. and Others, with Hints and Suggestions on Domestic Furniture and Decoration by William Watt.*

Ornament is diverse in origin. It ranges from classical moldings and medieval spindles to Renaissance putti. Sources vary from Oriental to New Eastern and from Moorish to Egyptian. Japanese art fosters two-dimensional designs (Nos. 116, 120).

Woods are exotic and decorative techniques are complex. Cherry is stained black and polished for simulating ebony. Bird's eye maple is popular. Bamboo is imported, and maple imitations repeat a Windsor style motif. Decoration is by shallow carving, marquetry, and inlaid woods and metals.

115. Clock, George Grant Elmslie and William Purcell, designers, Chicago, Illinois, for Niedecken Walbridge Company, Milwaukee, Wisconsin (documented), 1912 (documented); mahogany with brass and wood inlays. From the Henry B. Babson House, Riverside, Illinois. *The Art Institute of Chicago, gift of Mrs. Theodore D. Tiecken, Chicago, Illinois.*

116. Side Chair, Herter Brothers (attributed), New York City, 1876–1879; ebonized cherry. *The Art Institute of Chicago, Mrs. Alfred S. Burdick Fund, Chicago, Illinois.*

117. Armchair, Louis Comfort Tiffany and associates (documented), New York City, 1890; unidentified wood. Commissioned by Mr. and Mrs. H. O. Havemeyer, New York City. *The Shelburne Museum, Shelburne, Vermont.*

118. Chest of Drawers, New York City, 1874–1884; maple with cherry. Commissioned by Henry G. Marquand (1819–1902), New York City. *The Art Institute of Chicago, gift of the Antiquarian Society through the Mr. and Mrs. William Y. Hutchinson Fund, Chicago, Illinois.*

119. Bedstead, probably New York City, 1875–1885; maple. *The Metropolitan Museum of Art, purchase, Edgar J. Kaufmann Jr. Charitable Foundation Gift, 1969, New York, New York.*

120. Cabinet, Herter Brothers (incised stamp), New York City, 1876–1884; rosewood with cherry, maple, walnut, and satinwood. *The Art Institute of Chicago, gift of the Antiquarian Society through the Capital Campaign Fund, Chicago, Illinois.*

121

122

123

124

1. Glass door
2. Mirrored back panel
3. Relief-carved poppies
4. "Whiplash" curved lines
5. Gothic crocket as pendant
6. Medial and side stretcher
7. Form: Queen Anne style revival
8. Relief-carved flower buds
9. Cabriole leg

Americans usually associate the name with the curvilinear French movement. The sinuous curves of it often dominate form and decoration. Common motifs are naturalistic and stylized tulips, lilies, poppies, and leaves. The Art Nouveau style in furniture held limited appeal, and few examples survive.

An exposition at Paris in 1900 popularized the style internationally. It had originated in Paris, with encouragement by the art dealer Siegfried Bing. He featured it in his shop, known as the Maison de l'Art Nouveau, with other innovative movements, from the opening late in 1895 until the closing early in 1904. For Bing's clients, designers created costly handmade interpretations of their "Modern Art," which was inspired particularly by the curving line in Japanese art and French eighteenth-century Rococo art.

Sophisticated American furniture reveals influence of the Art Nouveau style, particularly in ornament, shortly before 1900 and until 1914. During this period, the style frequently influences curved lines in revival styles, and ornament occurs on mass-produced furniture as well as in the Arts and Crafts styles. There was a brief vogue for the style among furniture manufacturers from about 1900 to about 1903.

121. Cabinet, George C. Flint and Company (label), Chicago, Illinois, circa 1910; mahogany. *The Metropolitan Museum of Art, purchase, Edgar J. Kaufmann, Jr. Gift, 1968, New York, New York.*

122. Stand, United States, 1900–1915; mahogany. *The Margaret Woodbury Strong Museum, Rochester, New York.*

123. Side Chair, Charles Rohlfs (documented), designer, Buffalo, New York, circa 1898; oak. *The Art Museum, Princeton University, gift of Roland Rohlfs, Princeton, New Jersey.*

124. Corner Chair, probably New York City, 1900–1915; mahogany. *The Art Institute of Chicago, restricted gift of Dr. and Mrs. Edwin J. DeCosta, Chicago, Illinois.*

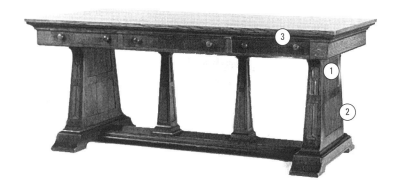

125

126

127

128

12

1. Relief carved tulip
2. Linenfold carving
3. Wooden drawer knobs
4. Ebony pegs covering screws
5. Inlays of abalone shell, silver, and copper
6. Splat in Chinese taste
7. Slip seat
8. Bracket in Chinese taste
9. Medial and side stretchers
10. Carved and painted panel drops for writing surface
11. Pewter and copper inlays
12. Leather upholstery

Handcraftsmanship, or its appearance, is a theme among individualistic approaches to furniture that are generally identified in America with the Arts and Crafts movement. Furniture usually is rectilinear and often offers a relationship between form and function. Ornament among different designers is Oriental, medieval, Renaissance, Gothic, or Art Nouveau in inspiration.

The Arts and Crafts movement evolved from British opinion that machines were lowering standards of form, decoration, and craftsmanship. Various efforts combining reform of the arts with reform of industrial society reached America with diverse results. William Morris is the apostle of the movement, though his private use of machines contradicts his public endorsements of crafts. The movement takes its name from the English organization known as the Arts and Crafts Exhibition Society. The first event in 1888 became a model for Americans, beginning with the first exhibition in San Francisco in 1896.

Solutions are individual, but the movement is national. Innovative architects in Illinois, encouraged by Frank Lloyd Wright, and in California by Charles and Henry Greene, designed furniture sympathetic with their buildings. George Niedecken in the Midwest, Lucia K. Mathews and Arthur F. Mathews on the West Coast, and Elbert Hubbard, with the brothers Gustav, Leopold, and J. George Stickley on the East Coast are among the diverse contributors to the movement. It encouraged efforts by amateurs, as well as professionals, because the prejudice was easing against people who worked with their hands.

Oak is a common wood. The use of it is a revival of an English and American material from the Medieval and Renaissance styles.

125. Library Table, design by George Washington Maher Firm (documented), Chicago, Illinois, 1905; oak. From the Emil Rudolph House, Highland Park, Illinois. *The Art Institute of Chicago, Robert R. McCormick Charitable Trust Fund, Chicago, Illinois.*

126. Serving Table, Charles Sumner Greene designer for Peter and John Hall workshop (documented), Pasadena, California, 1907–1909; mahogany with ebony pegs and inlays of silver, copper, and abalone. From the Robert R. Blacker House, Pasadena, California. *The Art Institute of Chicago, Wentworth Greene Field Memorial Fund and Maurice D. Galleher Fund, Chicago, Illinois.*

127. Side Chair, Charles Sumner Greene designer for Peter and John Hall workshop (documented), Pasadena, California, 1907–1909; mahogany with ebony pegs. From the Robert R. Blacker House, Pasadena, California. *The Art Institute of Chicago, restricted gift of the Graham Foundation, Chicago, Illinois.*

128. Desk, Lucia K. Mathews and Arthur F. Mathews, San Francisco, California, 1906–1918; walnut. *The Oakland Museum Association, gift of the Art Guild, Oakland, California.*

129. Rocking Chair, Harvey Ellis, designer for Gustav Stickley workshop (documented), Eastwood, New York, 1903; oak with pewter and copper inlays and leather upholstery. *The Art Institute of Chicago, gift of Mrs. Sidney Haskins, Chicago, Illinois.*

1. Caming
2. Colored and clear glass
3. Hinges
4. Leather upholstery
5. Blocks as design elements
6. Seat cantilever
7. Ball foot
8. Applied bands
9. Glass shades over electric light bulbs
10. Ogee, or cyma recta, molding

Furniture combines international innovation with architectural concerns of Frank Lloyd Wright and his disciples in the Midwestern Prairie School. Stained or fumed oak is favored. Craftsmanship varies from crude to skilled.

Basic themes in Wright's architecture recur in the furniture. Forms are rectilinear, include cantilevered elements, and stress horizontal lines. Surfaces are mostly unadorned. When ornament occurs, it is geometric and stylized. Wright and others encouraged use of machines in preparing materials and developing ornament.

Prairie School architects designed furniture for harmony between a building and its furnishings. But without evidence, furniture cannot be attributed to an architect for a building. Wright's firm, for example, designed some furniture, but his reliance on staff or craftsmen for it is unknown. Equally uncertain is his participation in designs by the firm of George M. Niedecken and John S. Walbridge that received Wright's commissions for several interiors. Niedecken, the partner active as a designer, had been closely associated with Wright and understood his concepts. Even he worked independently on some projects: He used classical moldings on a desk for Wright's Coonley House during a period in which Wright had abandoned such details (No. 134).

Many sources abroad inspired design elements in furniture associated with the Prairie School. The English Arts and Crafts movement is the general background. Specific features of various forms originate in the contemporary European centers of innovative design. They range from tall backs on chairs, for example, in the designs of Charles Rennie Mackintosh of Scotland to the affinity of modular decoration in Purcell, Elmslie, and Feick's chair to one by Koloman Moser of Austria (No. 132). The means of transmission often are difficult to trace in an era of convenient travel, photographs, and publications.

130. Screen, frame by George M. Niedecken (label), glass production by Linden Glass Company (attributed), glass design by Frank Lloyd Wright (attributed); Milwaukee, Wisconsin, and Chicago, Illinois, 1902–1907; oak and glass. Frame includes a bronze plaque which states: "The Art and Craft of the Machine/A Lecture by Frank Lloyd Wright/Hull House March 6, 1901/Chicago Arts and Crafts Society." *The Art Institute of Chicago, gift of Mr. and Mrs. F. M. Fahernwald, by exchange, Chicago, Illinois.*

131. Side Chair, Frank Lloyd Wright Firm, designer (documented), Chicago, Illinois, 1904 (documented); oak with leather upholstery. From the Larkin Building, Buffalo, New York. *The Art Institute of Chicago, Bessie Bennett Fund, Chicago, Illinois.*

132. Armchair, William Gray Purcell, George Feick, and George Grant Elmslie Firm, designers (documented), Milwaukee, Wisconsin, 1911–1912; oak with leather upholstery. From the Merchants Bank, Winona, Minnesota. *The Art Institute of Chicago, Fern and Manfred Steinfeld Fund, Chicago, Illinois.*

133. Side Chair, George Grant Elmslie, designer (attributed), Chicago, Illinois, circa 1910; oak. Patron unknown. *The Art Institute of Chicago, gift of the Antiquarian Society through Mrs. William P. Boggess II, Chicago, Illinois.*

134. Desk, Niedecken Walbridge Company, designer (documented), Milwaukee, Wisconsin, circa 1910; oak. From the Avery Coonley House, Riverside, Illinois. *The Art Institute of Chicago, gift of The Graham Foundation for Advanced Studies in the Fine Arts, Chicago, Illinois.*

135

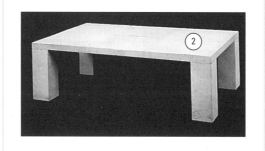

136

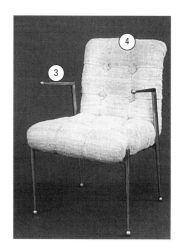

137

138

139

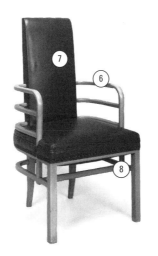

140

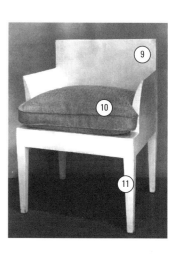

Art Deco Styles, 1925–1945

Controlled curves or crisp angles, monumental or delicate forms, and traditional wood or innovative steel are features of the greatly varying Art Deco movement in design. Common themes among the variations are simplicity of shape, emphasis on planes, and smooth surfaces.

Known to contemporaries as "Modern," the styles of the period are broadly identified today as "Art Deco." The term is derived from the Parisian event of 1925 that popularized the shift in taste and was titled "l'Exposition Internationale des Arts Décoratives et Industriels Modernes."

The immediate result of the exposition was a style of attenuated forms, lavish veneers, and boldly contrasting inlays in the tradition that Eliel Saarinen commanded. Americans were equally open to other influences. Design gradually shifted in quality furniture of the 1930s to clarity of form as differently expressed as in the designs of Donald Deskey or Samuel Marx. Use of metal and experiments with construction reveal influences from the contemporary International Style abroad.

Fine craftsmanship and lavish materials are features of quality furniture. Surfaces vary from veneers and inlays of unusual woods to lacquer, parchment, and glass. The cocktail table is an innovation, chair backs are low and high, and upholstery varies from restrained and smooth to opulent and textured.

135. Armchair, Donald Deskey, designer (documented), New York City, 1932 (documented); mahogany with leather upholstery. *Radio City Music Hall Productions, Inc., New York, New York.*

136. Cocktail Table, Samuel Marx (documented), designer for William Quigley Company (documented), Chicago, Illinois, 1944 (documented); white leather over unidentified wood. From the Leigh B. Block apartment, Chicago, Illinois. *The Art Institute of Chicago, gift of Leigh B. Block, Chicago, Illinois.*

137. Armchair, Donald Deskey (documented), designer for the Royal Chrome Company (documented), New York City, circa 1938; steel, with original wool upholstery, by Dorothy Liebes (documented). From the Samuel Marx apartment, Chicago, Illinois. *The Art Institute of Chicago, gift of Mrs. Florene Schoenborn, Chicago, Illinois.*

138. Dining Table, Eliel Saarinen (doucmented), designer for the Company of Master Craftsmen (documented), Bloomfield Hills, Michigan, 1930 (documented); hare, ebony, box, and holly woods. *The Cranbrook Academy of Art and Museum, Bloomfield Hills, Michigan.*

139. Armchair, Kem Weber (documented), designer for the Grand Rapids Chair Company (documented), Grand Rapids, Michigan, 1928–1929 (documented); unidentified woods with green shellac and red leather upholstery. *The Art Institute of Chicago, Fern and Manfred Steinfeld Fund, Chicago, Illinois.*

140. Armchair, Hammond Kroll (documented), designer, New York City, circa 1935; parchment over wood, with original wool cushion, woven by Helen Kroll Kramer (documented). *The Smithsonian Institution, the Cooper-Hewitt National Museum of Design, gift of Helen Kroll Kramer in memory of Dr. Milton Lurie, New York, New York.*

141

142

143

144

145

146

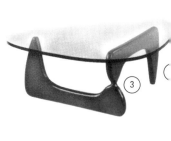

1. Molded laminated woods
2. Medial and side stretchers
3. Base pivot
4. Black shellac
5. Molded plastic
6. Cast aluminum

Industrial materials and industrial production meet objectives of furniture independent of traditional styles. The concept originated in Europe after World War I with indirect sources in the furniture Reform movement of England.

The Bauhaus, a school founded in 1919 in Germany at Weimar and later moved to Dessau and Berlin, became the center of the new movement in the 1920s through Walter Gropius, Ludwig Miës van der Rohe, and Marcel Breuer. These leaders of the Bauhaus and other immigrants in the 1930s established the approach in American design.

The Museum of Modern Art encouraged the movement in 1940 with a competition for domestic furnishings. Eero Saarinen and Charles Eames won first prizes for a chair design and standardized tables and case furniture. The revolutionary chair combined seat, back, and arms into one unit of laminated woods formed in a mold. The design potential was realized after World War II, when Saarinen and Eames remained leaders in the movement for industrially produced furniture in plastic, plywood, and metal. Each advanced the innovative material and construction of mass-produced plastic shells for seating and other elements.

Breuer's intent and that of other Europeans in the 1920s and 1930s was furniture without "style." But furniture designed in the International Style clearly reveals different aesthetic preferences among designers, as well as the influence of other contemporary movements in the arts. Abstract form in painting and sculpture by Joan Miró, for example, influence furniture shapes by the Eames staff and Noguchi.

141. Armchair, Harry Bertoia, designer for Knoll International (documented), East Greenville, Pennsylvania, 1956; steel with vinyl upholstery. *The Art Institute of Chicago, gift of Malcolm, Kay, Kim, and Kyle Kamin, Chicago, Illinois.*

142. Side Chair, Charles Eames Office (documented), designer for Evans Products Company, Plymouth, Michigan, 1947–1949; laminated woods. *The Art Institute of Chicago, gift of Mrs. Eugene A. Davidson, Chicago, Illinois.*

143. Armchair, Eero Saarinen (documented), designer for Knoll International, East Greenville, Pennsylvania, 1956; plastic, aluminum. *The Art Institute of Chicago, gift of Knoll International, Chicago, Illinois.*

144. Rocking Chair for Child, Charles Eames Office (documented), designer for Herman Miller Company, Zeeland, Michigan, 1953; fiberglass, steel, birch. *The Art Institute of Chicago, gift of Joseph H. Makler, Chicago, Illinois.*

145. Cocktail Table, George Nelson (documented), designer for Herman Miller Company, Zeeland, Michigan, 1963; chrome and glass. *The Art Institute of Chicago, gift of Malcolm, Kay, Kim, and Kyle Kamin, Chicago, Illinois.*

146. Armchair (Womb Chair), Eero Saarinen (documented), designer for Knoll International, East Greenville, Pennsylvania, 1948; cowhide upholstery over plastic shell. *The Art Institute of Chicago, gift of Mrs. Alfred H. Newman, Chicago, Illinois.*

147. Cocktail Table, Isamu Noguchi (documented), designer for Herman Miller Company, Zeeland, Michigan, 1944; birch and glass. *The Art Institute of Chicago, gift of Malcolm, Kay, Kim, and Kyle Kamin, Chicago, Illinois.*

148

149

150

151

152

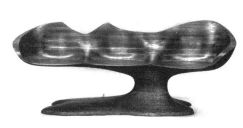

Execution varies from a craftsman personally creating unique furniture to his supervising others in making his designs. Iron or plastics are occasional materials, but the general concern is with traditional wood. Patrons mainly commission furniture for domestic use.

The movement has evolved nationally since the late 1940s. It is a reaction to standardized industrial furniture, and it continues the philosophy of personal expression from the Arts and Crafts period. Wharton Esherick is a link to craftsmen and their ideals at the turn of the twentieth century through his example from the 1920s to the 1960s. Over his career, he gradually shifted from craftsman to designer and administrator for a workshop.

Personal styles reflect greatly varying intellectual and emotional responses to furniture as a practical or even a humorous element in daily life. Forms may be rectilinear, abstract, or occasionally anthropomorphic and biomorphic. Some designers and craftsmen have turned to historic styles for inspiration.

Woods may be selected for uniformity of color and grain, chosen for irregularities, or laminated for the potential of form, strength, and decoration. Production is equally diverse. It may rely on hand craftsmanship or modern technology in any phase of preparing, forming, and finishing woods.

148. Table entitled *Demi-Lune Table*, Wendell Castle, designer (documented) and John Zanetti craftsman (label), Scottsville, New York, 1985; rosewood with ziricote veneer on top and ivory for inlay and feet. *The Art Institute of Chicago, Raymond W. Garbe Fund in honor of Carl A. Erickson, Sr., Chicago, Illinois.*

149. Looking Glass, Daniel K. Jackson (label), Philadelphia, Pennsylvania, 1973 (documented); rosewood, Osage orange. *The Philadelphia Museum of Art, gift of the Friends of the Philadelphia Museum of Art, Philadelphia, Pennsylvania.*

150. Double Music Rack, Wharton Esherick (documented), Paoli, Pennsylvania, 1962; walnut, cherry. *The Wharton Esherick Museum, Paoli, Pennsylvania.*

151. Cradle-cabinet, Sam Maloof (label), Alta Loma, California, 1968; laminated walnut. *American Craft Museum, gift of the Johnson Wax Company to the American Craft Museum through the American Craft Council, New York, New York.*

152. Chest-table, Wharton Esherick (label), Paoli, Pennsylvania, 1969; walnut. *The American Craft Museum, gift of the Johnson Wax Company to the American Craft Museum through the American Craft Council, New York, New York.*

153. Sofa, Wendell Castle (label), Scottsville, New York, 1967; laminated oak. From the Lee Nordness apartment, New York City. *The Art Institute of Chicago, gift of Karen Johnson Boyd, Chicago, Illinois.*

154

155

156

157

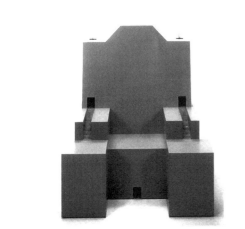

158

1

Contemporary Styles, 1981–Present

Challenges to the International style prevailing since the 1950s gradually gained a public through a movement among the American artists designing furniture for personal use and the influence of Italian design in the 1970s. The rebellion crystallized in 1981 with designs by an Italian collaboration known as Memphis. Named for the city in the United States, it included such Americans as Peter Shire. Furniture rarely is mass produced. Practicality is secondary to aesthetics.

Approaches greatly differ among designers. One theme is reversing principles of the International Style. Function does not determine form as in Albert Paley's bench (No. 154). Colors are the rule, not the exception, and unusual combinations are typical. Surface patterns are embraced, not omitted. History is teased, instead of revered, as in Venturi's version of a chair in the Queen Anne style (No. 156; compare with No. 24).

Popular culture is another source of the new aesthetic. Pop Art became a theme in American painting and sculpture during the early 1960s but was dormant by the 1970s. Lee Payne's *Neopolitan Table* forcefully represents the recurrence of the theme in the 1980s through the reference to a block of chocolate, vanilla, and strawberry ice cream (No. 158).

Many objects offer whimsical or overtly irrational elements, which parallel the contemporary revival of surrealism in painting and sculpture. Lewis & Clark envision the godlike occupant of their *Temple Chair* activating unseen ceremonies of an imaginary cult (No. 157). The *Phidias Chair* is Peter Shire's essay in geometric forms dramatized by the impression of precarious balance (No. 159). Wendell Castle's giant hooks support the top of *Lucky Table* that is carved to seem warped and impractical (No. 155).

Emotional response is the designer's objective. Changes in the usual form, scale, color, texture, surface pattern, or concept often are meant to shock the viewer into a new awareness.

154. Bench; Albert Paley, designer and maker (documented); Rochester, New York, 1994 (documented); forged steel and mahogany. *The Victoria and Albert Museum, London, England.*

155. *Lucky Table,* Wendell Castle, designer and craftsman (documented), Scottsville, New York, 1986 (documented); stained and painted cherry and curly maple veneer. *The Art Institute of Chicago, Raymond W. Garbe Fund in honor of Carl A. Erickson, Sr., Chicago, Illinois.*

156. Side Chair, Robert Venturi, designer (documented), for Knoll International, 1984 (documented); laminated plywood and plastic. *The Art Institute of Chicago, gift of Mr. Marshall Cogan and Knoll International Holdings, Inc., Chicago, Illinois. (Photograph: Courtesy of Knoll International.)*

157. *Temple Chair,* Lewis & Clark (James Angivine Lewis and Clark Edward Ellefson), Columbia, South Carolina, 1983 (documented); Colorcore Formica on various woods. *The Art Institute of Chicago, gift of the Formica Corporation, Chicago, Illinois.*

158. *Neopolitan Table,* Lee Payne (documented), Atlanta, Georgia, 1983 (documented); Colorcore Formica on various woods. *The Art Institute of Chicago, gift of Lee Payne, Chicago, Illinois.*

159. *Phidias Chair,* Peter Shire (documented); designer, Los Angeles, California, 1984 (documented); baked enamel on steel. *The Oakland Museum, Rena Bransten Fund, Oakland, California.*

160

161

162

163

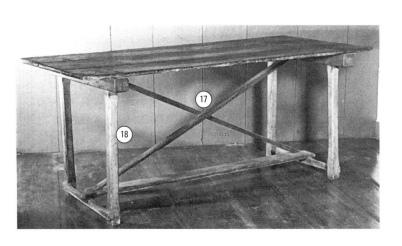

Dutch Style, 1624–1860

1. Ovolo molding with raised panels
2. Fielded panels
3. Boss
4. Drawer
5. Ball foot
6. Finial
7. Blue-green paint
8. Flat arm rest
9. Turned support
10. Rush seat
11. Cornice
12. Black, gray, white decoration
13. Back tilts for table
14. Seat lifts for storage
15. Medial stretcher
16. Trestle base
17. Cross stretchers
18. Chamfered corner

Seventeenth-century immigrants to Dutch claims in the mid-Atlantic region introduced furniture designs continuing in isolated areas in northern New Jersey, on Long Island, and in the Hudson River Valley long after the major settlement of New Amsterdam became the prominent English community of New York City. Diverse origins of the colonists from the Netherlands and their equally diverse sophistication are evident in the recorded furniture.

The practical *kast,* common in northern Europe during the seventeenth century for storing clothing, linens, and other personal articles, is a major form. It survives in many variations. They range from seventeenth-century versions in oak and eighteenth-century examples in walnut, maple, or tulip with painted decoration, to early nineteenth-century mahogany examples with inlays in the Federal style.

Other furniture forms and their decoration also reveal Continental influences. Turnings are elaborate on chairs and tables. Curves are complex on cupboards or other forms, such as the multipurpose chair-table with a storage compartment beneath the chair seat and a back lowering to become a table top. Simple tables include stretchers between legs as well as central diagonal braces between top and base. Furniture often is finished with paint or stain in red, blue, or gray.

160. *Kast* (Wardrobe), New York City area, 1676–1700; red oak with walnut trim. *The Art Institute of Chicago, Sanford Fund, Chicago, Illinois.*

161. Armchair, Kings County, Queens County, or New York City, 1681–1700; oak painted blue-green. *The Art Institute of Chicago, Sewell L. Avery Fund, Chicago, Illinois.*

162. *Kast* (Wardrobe), New York City area, 1700–1735; yellow poplar with black, gray, white painted decoration. *The Henry Francis du Pont Winterthur Museum, Winterthur, Delaware.*

163. Chair-table, Hudson River Valley, 1690–1740; maple oak. *The Art Institute of Chicago, gift of Jamee J. and Marshall Field, in honor of Nancy J. and Milo M. Naeve, Chicago, Illinois.*

164. Table, Hudson River Valley, 1725–1775; maple and poplar painted gray. *Historic Hudson Valley, van Cortlandt Manor House, Tarrytown, New York.*

165

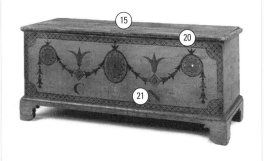

166

168

169

167

German Style, 1751–1870

Germanic immigrants from central Europe to New York, North Carolina, and southeastern Pennsylvania introduced a style flourishing by the late eighteenth century. Immigration to Virginia and Ohio from earlier settlements and abroad introduced Germanic culture to other regions. The Germans initially continued seventeenth- and eighteenth-century forms abroad for chairs, chests, tables, and other furniture. American variations of Germanic decorations soon were adapted to traditional chests, boxes, and wardrobes known as *shonks,* as well as to such English forms as chests of drawers, clocks, and desks with bookcases. The German style flourished through the early nineteenth century. It lost vigor at mid-century with the dissipation of German culture and access to mass-produced furniture.

Storage chests of tulip wood for men and women are the favored form. Elaborate versions are brightly painted in red, blue, white, yellow with images of tulips, hearts, birds, stars, and unicorns. Walnut inlaid with white sulphur designs of scrolls, pilasters, hearts, and shells are a distinctive and smaller group. Names and initials of owners and commemorative dates frequently document pride of possession.

165. *Shonk* (Wardrobe), Oley area, Pennsylvania, 1790; tulip with blue, white, red painted decoration. *The Art Institute of Chicago, Elizabeth R. Vaughan Fund, Chicago, Illinois.*

166. Side Chair, Zoar, Ohio, circa 1817–1837; chestnut and oak. *The Art Institute of Chicago, restricted gift of Jamee J. And Marshall Field and Mr. and Mrs. John Trumbull; Sewell L. Avery and Elizabeth Vaughan Funds; and Charles F. Montgomery and Charlotte Olson, by exchange, Chicago, Illinois.*

167. Desk and Bookcase, eastern Pennsylvania, 1785–1810; pine, painted blue-green and white. *The Henry Francis du Pont Winterthur Museum, Winterthur, Delaware.*

168. Chest, Ephrata area, Pennsylvania, 1783; walnut with sulphur inlay. *The Smithsonian Institution, Washington, D.C.*

169. Chest, Albany or Schoharie Counties, New York, 1807–1816; white pine. *Gift of the Antiquarian Society through the Juli and David Grainger Fund, Chicago, Illinois.*

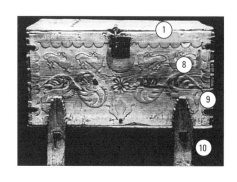

170

171

172

173

174

17

1. Hinged top
2. Triangle motif
3. Fielded panel with relief carving
4. Channel molding
5. Exposed mortise-and-tenon joint
6. Spindles
7. Hinged door with spindles
8. Relief-carved lions, rabbits, foliate scrolls
9. Exposed dovetail joint
10. Separate stand
11. Indian stepped design symbolizes heaven and rain
12. Relief-carved panels of lions, rosettes, pomegranates
13. Batten

Furniture was rare in Spanish territories across the present southern United States. Surviving examples are mainly from New Mexico, where scarce tools, hinges, and locks were imported about 2,000 miles overland from Mexico City.

Santa Fe was in founded in 1610, and life there was simple. Beyond the capital, it was primitive. Until the nineteenth century, tables, chairs, benches, and beds were unknown except for those in churches or prosperous households. The earliest survivals are from the eighteenth century and continue traditions for simple furniture in seventeenth- and eighteenth-century Spain.

Chests are the common form. They rest on the floor, on stands, or on legs. The other traditional forms are *alacenas* (wall cupboards), *repisos* (shelves), *tarmitas* (stools), and *trasteros* (cupboards). Furniture is made according to multiples or segments of the *vara*, the Spanish unit of measure equal to thirty-three inches.

Decoration is simple. Chests, cupboards, and shelves include geometric designs or generalized motifs, such as flowers, shells, rosettes, scrolls, and occasionally animals. Motifs are carved in relief or painted in yellow, red, blue, black, and white. Grooves and chip carving are common.

Soft Ponderosa pine is the principal wood. The difficulty of preparing it, before the introduction of sawmills in 1846, resulted in reworking parts from worn or damaged furniture.

170. Chest, possibly by Francisco A. Valdez, Taos-Santa Cruz Area, New Mexico, circa 1812; Ponderosa pine. From the Ranchos de Taos Church. *The Art Institute of Chicago, restricted gift of Warren L. Batts, Wesley M. Dixon, Jr., Jamee J. and Marshall Field, Mrs. Frank L. Sulzberger, and an anonymous donor in honor of Nelson E. Smyth, Chicago, Illinois.*

171. Armchair, northern New Mexico 1776–1800; Ponderosa Pine. *Museum of New Mexico, Santa Fe, New Mexico. (Negative No. 25647.)*

172. Food Cupboard, northern New Mexico, 1800–1850; Ponderosa pine. *The American Museum in Britain, Claverton Manor, Bath, England.*

173. Chest with Stand, northern New Mexico 1781–1800; Ponderosa pine. *Museum of New Mexico, Santa Fe, New Mexico. (Negative No. 65701.)*

174. Arm Chair, Santa Fe area, New Mexico, 1776–1821; Ponderosa pine. *The Art Institute of Chicago, restricted gift of Mr. and Mrs. Robert A. Kubicek, Chicago, Illinois.*

175. Chest, northern New Mexico, 1781–1820; Ponderosa pine. *The American Museum in Britain, Claverton Manor, Bath, England.*

1. Hinged top with battens
2. Relief-carved tulips, leaves, hearts
3. Side rail
4. Rail
5. Stile
6. Knob handle
7. Cornice
8. Scallop shell
9. Ogee molding
10. Serpentine scroll
11. Cabriole leg
12. Square pad foot
13. Hinged leaf
14. "Butterfly" leaf support
15. Splay leg
16. Double baluster turning
17. Stretcher
18. Worn ball foot
19. Finial
20. Turned posts
21. Cyma curve
22. Concave arm for tying child
23. Footrest
24. Crest rail with yoke
25. Concave, urn-shaped splat
26. Side, medial, and back stretchers
27. Leaf-carving at knee
28. Trifid foot with raised panels
29. Chinese fret
30. Side rail
31. Front rail
32. Claw-and-ball foot

Furniture in many traditions includes six-board chests and trestle tables of the Medieval style, joined and turned forms, modifications of sophisticated styles, or is new in concept. Spanish, Dutch, and German immigrants evolved other traditions, forming distinct styles.

Significant among designs original to America are late seventeenth-century dower chests, carved in low relief with tulips, hearts, and other motifs popular in the isolated Connecticut River Valley. They are known as "Hadley" chests—after the town of Hadley, Massachusetts—but craftsmen made them over several generations from Hartford, Connecticut, to Deerfield, Massachusetts (No. 176).

Tables occur in many variations. One is known today as the "butterfly" type for the shape of the leaf supports (No. 178).

Common chairs follow a European tradition of shaped slats and turned legs introduced in America during the seventeenth century. The many variations range from high backs in New England—influenced by chairs of the William and Mary style—to walnut chairs delicate in appearance, yet sturdy in construction, from Pennsylvania.

Adaptations of sophisticated furniture may be contemporary with a style or may combine motifs from earlier styles. Furniture may be decorated with simple carving and painted.

Woods usually are local. Birch and maple often are stained imitations of mahogany.

176. Chest ("Hadley" type), Connecticut River Valley, 1671–1720; oak, white pine. *The Art Institute of Chicago, gift of Robert R. McCormick Charitable Trust, Chicago, Illinois.*

177. Chest-on-chest, on Frame, possibly by Samuel Dunlap, New Hampshire, 1781–1820; maple. *The Currier Gallery of Art, Manchester, New Hampshire.*

178. Table ("butterfly" type), Connecticut or western Massachusetts, 1711–1740; cherry and maple, painted red. *Historic Deerfield, Inc., Deerfield, Massachusetts.*

179. Armchair (Great Chair), Norwich or Lebanon, Connecticut, 1671–1710; ash and maple. *The Art Institute of Chicago, Wesley M. Dixon, Jr. Fund, Chicago, Illinois.*

180. Highchair for Child, Pennsylvania, 1741–1775; walnut. *The Art Institute of Chicago, gift of the Barker Welfare Foundation, Chicago, Illinois.*

181. Side Chair, William Savery (attributed), Philadelphia, Pennsylvania, 1746–1760; maple. *The Art Institute of Chicago, gift of the Antiquarian Society, Chicago, Illinois.*

182. Side Chair, Eliphalet or Aaron Chapin, East Windsor or Hartford, Connecticut, circa 1771–1790; mahogany with white pine and yellow pine. *The Art Institute of Chicago, gift of the Antiquarian Society, Chicago, Illinois.*

183

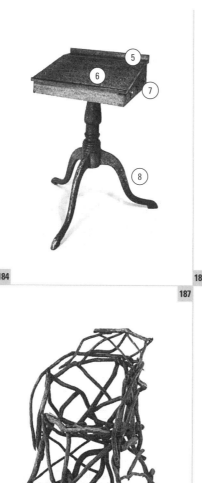

184

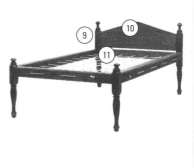

185

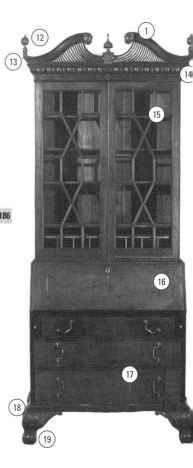

186

187

188

1. Broken-arch pediment
2. Face (dial and spandrels)
3. Red and brown paint
4. Scalloped apron in Queen Anne style
5. Yellow and brown paint
6. Writing surface
7. Drawers
8. Cabriole leg of Queen Anne style
9. Low-post bedstead (wooden frame)
10. Headboard
11. Rope
12. Finial
13. Ovolo molding with egg-and-dart motif
14. Blind Chinese fret
15. Muntin
16. Inlaid festoon in Federal style
17. Serpentine curve
18. Two relief-carved scallop shells of Queen Anne style
19. Claw-and-ball foot of Chippendale style
20. Hickory with bark intact
21. Shaped oak back and seat

The great variety of the eighteenth century gradually decreases with developing mass production. By the 1870s, factories replace the efforts of most local craftsmen.

The early-nineteenth century includes variations of many styles. Chests and tables still occur in the Medieval style. Simple beds follow the seventeenth- and eighteenth-century form. Descendants of Spanish, Dutch, and German immigrants continue their distinctive styles. Adaptations of the Queen Anne, Chippendale, and Federal styles continue in isolated areas. Shakers produce simple designs into the early-nineteenth century in their distinctive style.

Designs are carved with less frequency as training and skills decline. Decoration increasingly is achieved by red, blue, yellow, or white paint, by simulating mahogany and maple grains, or by working simple designs into wet paint. By the 1830s, stencil decoration is common. Chairs by the Hitchcock factory and others gradually complement those in the Windsor style, as furniture production becomes an industry.

Rustic furniture of tree limbs with bark intact evolves in the mid-nineteenth century as one of the styles for furniture in rural areas, mountain lodges, or informal rooms.

183. Clock, Silas Hoadley (label), Plymouth, Connecticut, 1813–circa 1823; white pine painted red and brown. *The Art Institute of Chicago, gift of Marshall Field, Charles C. Haffner III, Mrs. Burton W. Hales, Mrs. C. Phillip Miller, Mrs. Clyde Runnells, and Mrs. Frank L. Sulzberger, Chicago, Illinois.*

184. Writing Stand, New England, 1815–1840; maple and white pine painted yellow and brown. *The Art Institute of Chicago, Bessie Bennett Fund, Chicago, Illinois.*

185. Bedstead, Massachusetts, 1800–1850; ash. *The Henry Francis du Pont Winterthur Museum, gift of Joseph Downs, Winterthur, Delaware.*

186. Desk and Bookcase, John Shearer (signed), Martinsburg, West Virginia, 1801; cherry, walnut, oak, mulberry. *The Museum of Early Southern Decorative Arts, Winston-Salem, North Carolina.*

187. Armchair, northeastern United States, 1891–1910; various woods. *The Art Institute of Chicago, restricted gift of Jeffrey Shedd, Chicago, Illinois.*

188. Rocking Chair, southern Ohio, 1890–1910; hickory frame, oak seat, back, and rockers. *The Art Institute of Chicago, gift of Mr. and Mrs. Robert A. Kubicek, Chicago, Illinois.*

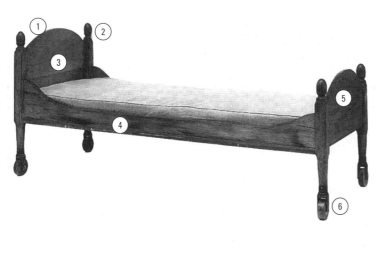

189

190

191

192

19

1. Low-post bedstead (wooden frame)
2. Acorn-shaped finial
3. Headboard
4. Side rail
5. Footboard
6. Maple wheel
7. Drawer with knob handle
8. Slide for work surface
9. Bracket foot of Queen Anne style
10. Cabriole leg of Queen Anne style
11. Slat back
12. Splint seat
13. Rush seat

Efficient design and effective craftsmanship support principles of the United Society of Believers in Christ's Second Appearing. In 1774, nine members of the celibate sect that would become known as "Shakers," because of movements during ritual dances in their worship, came to America from England. Conversions reached a peak in the 1840s with about 6,000 members in communal centers from New England and the South to the Midwest.

Shaker furniture design generally follows early-nineteenth-century simple traditions familiar to the membership. Shakers made most of their furniture for dormitories and workshops, but in Mount Lebanon, New York, they made chairs and stools for public sale in the late-nineteenth and early-twentieth centuries. Later furniture also includes simplified motifs from sophisticated styles.

Shaker practicality encourages such features as low-backed chairs that could be stored under dining tables, wheels on beds, and storage drawers built into walls. Early furniture is painted. By the mid-nineteenth century, stains, clear varnish, and shellac enhance grain and color of woods, which are functional as well as decorative. Easily shaped hickory or oak serves as chair slats, durable maple for drawer knobs, and dense cherry for table tops. Other woods include butternut, chestnut, pear, and walnut, as well as easily worked pine. Slight differences between various Shaker workshops are particularly evident in chairs through finial design, number and design of slats, and the varied use of straw, reed, or tape for seats.

189. Bedstead, Mount (New) Lebanon, New York, Shaker Community (documented), 1801–1830; chestnut posts, pine footboard, headboard, and rails, maple wheels. *The Henry Francis du Pont Winterthur Museum, gift of Miss Helen Brown, Miss Margaret Brown, and Miss Pauline Brown, Winterthur, Delaware.*

190. Desk, unidentified Shaker Community, United States, 1801–1850; ash, pine, *The Henry Francis du Pont Winterthur Museum, Winterthur, Delaware.*

191. Stand, attributed to Enfield, Connecticut, Shaker Community, 1791–1830. *The Henry Francis du Pont Winterthur Museum, Winterthur, Delaware.*

192. Rocking Chair, attributed to Mount (New) Lebanon, New York, Shaker Community, 1801–1830; birch, maple. *The Henry Francis du Pont Winterthur Museum, Winterthur, Delaware; gift of The Halcyon Foundation, The American Museum in Britain, Claverton Manor, Bath, England.*

193. Dining Chair, Mount (New) Lebanon, New York, Shaker Community (label), 1873–circa 1883; maple. *The Art Institute of Chicago, gift of the Antiquarian Society through the Mrs. Len H. Small Fund, Chicago, Illinois.*

194

195

196

197

198

19

Windsor Style, 1750–Present

Windsor furniture parts interlock for strength through tension. Side chairs complement armchairs by the 1770s, and settees are popular by the 1790s. Stools and tables are occasional. Construction is revolutionized by fitting interchangeable parts into plank seats instead of securing the seat to a continuous element forming leg and stile. Mass production is achieved by volume production of parts, which are stored until assembled.

Woods selected for function include hard oak for arms or crests, dense maple for legs, supple hickory and birch for spindles or crests, and soft ash, tulip, or pine for shaped seats. By the mid-nineteenth century, wood color and grain are decorative features, instead of red, yellow, blue-green or white paint for disguising grain or color of various woods and for protection from weather and wear. Rare eighteenth-century Windsors with cabriole legs and pad feet are made of walnut, a wood recurring in the mid-twentieth century.

Craftsmen specialize in Windsors until the early nineteenth century, by making or buying interchangeable parts. After nineteenth-century factory production, independent craftsmen return in the mid-twentieth century.

Windsor furniture evolved in or near London between 1710 and 1720. A credible tradition asserts that the name derives from use as garden furniture at Windsor Castle. Rural English craftsmen were developing the style by the second quarter of the eighteenth century, and it reached Philadelphia at mid-century. By the Revolution, variations occur in New York City and Newport. After the Revolution, craftsmen made Windsors throughout the new nation, and the furniture is common for elegant, as well as simple, houses and for gardens. Decorative turnings are baluster shapes in the eighteenth century, bamboo shapes after the Revolution, concentric rings in the mid-nineteenth century; they disappear in the twentieth.

194. Windsor Armchair, Philadelphia, Pennsylvania, 1761–1770; tulip seat, maple legs, hickory spindles, oak arms, painted blue-green. *The Art Institute of Chicago, gift of Elizabeth R. Vaughan, Chicago, Illinois.*

195. Windsor Armchair, Philadelphia, Pennsylvania, 1761–1775; walnut. *The Art Institute of Chicago, gift of Joyce Martin Brown, Marshall Field, Mrs. Harold T. Martin, Melinda Martin Vance, and Mary Waller Langhorne Fund, Chicago, Illinois.*

196. Windsor Settee, probably Pennsylvania, 1786–1800; oak spindles, crest rail, arms, tulip seat, maple legs, stretchers, and rear stiles; painted brown over red and blue-green. *The Yale University Art Gallery, Mabel Brady Garvan Collection, New Haven, Connecticut.*

197. Windsor Rocking Chair, New England, 1831–1850; hickory or oak spindles, pine seat, maple legs and arms, painted brown and red with gilt stencil decoration. *Greenfield Village and Henry Ford Museum, Dearborn, Michigan. (Accession No. 24. III. 120.)*

198. Windsor Side Chair for Child, probably New England, 1881–1890; oak rail, ash seat, birch spindles. *Mark Twain Memorial, Hartford, Connecticut.*

199. Windsor Side Chair, George Nakashima, New Hope, Pennsylvania (documented), 1988 (design introduced circa 1962); walnut with hickory spindles. *The Art Institute of Chicago, Raymond W. Garbe fund in honor of Carl A. Erickson, Sr., Chicago, Illinois.*

200

201

202

203

204

205

2

Garden Furniture Styles, 1801–1914

Windsors grace gardens and houses until the early nineteenth century. Chairs made in factories replace Windsors indoors by mid-century as other furniture became available for outdoors.

Iron production had greatly advanced from the late-eighteenth to the mid-nineteenth centuries in England. Costs were reduced and casting improved for delicacy in details and greater size in parts. Legs, backs, and seats could be made as standard parts, shipped, and assembled with screws. Occasional furniture in the Gothic style introduced widespread production of tables, chairs, and settees in the Rococo Revival style. General popularity led to designs in all of the later styles. They were disseminated from England and within America, as the product of one manufacturer easily served as the pattern for another's mold.

Wire production encouraged a new kind of furniture by the 1870s. Interlaced designs provided both strength and decoration in chairs, stands, and settees.

Native willow and imported rattan offered materials for a wide range of simple and elaborate forms after the War Between the States. The furniture also served informally in houses by the late nineteenth and early twentieth centuries.

Rustic furniture of gnarled tree limbs with the bark intact gained popularity at mid-century with the Naturalistic style. Most of the survivals are from the late nineteenth century, when the approach became common, not only in gardens, but also in mountain lodges and in vernacular furniture throughout the United States.

200. Settee, Washington Irving, designer (documented), circa 1836; cast iron. West Point Foundry, Cold Spring, New York (documented); *Historic Hudson Valley, Sunnyside, Tarrytown, New York.*

201. Side Chair, Robert Wood and Company (label), Philadelphia, Pennsylvania, 1851–1860; cast iron. *Greenfield Village and Henry Ford Museum, Dearborn, Michigan. (Accession No. 65. 118. 3.)*

202. Table, United States, 1851–1870; cast iron. *The Metropolitan Museum of Art, purchase, Edgar J. Kauffman, Jr. Foundation Gift, 1968, New York, New York.*

203. Urn, Van Dorn Iron Works, Cleveland, Ohio, 1851–1885; cast iron. *The Metropolitan Museum of Art, purchase, Edgar J. Kaufmann, Jr. Foundation Gift, 1969, New York, New York.*

204. Settee, Colt Willow Ware Works, Hartford, Connecticut, circa 1853–1873; willow. *The Wadsworth Atheneum, Bequest of Elizabeth Hart Jarvis Colt, Hartford, Connecticut.*

205. Side Chair, United States, 1875–1880; wire. *Greenfield Village and Henry Ford Museum, Dearborn, Michigan. (Accession No. 58. 57. 1.).*

206. Settee, Kramer Brothers (label), Dayton Ohio, 1905–1925; cast iron. *The Art Institute of Chicago, gift of the Antiquarian Society through Mrs. Burton W. Hales, Chicago, Illinois.*

Publications in the following list are selective but include the major references available in English in the United States for style, technology, and terminology. They are arranged in two general categories: **Periodicals** and **Books, Articles, and Manuscripts.** In the latter category, articles may be from journals and magazines cited among the **Periodicals,** but they are listed separately for their significance to the theme of this book. Annotations occur either to clarify the scope of a publication or to alert the reader to unusual circumstances.

The category of **Books, Articles, and Manuscripts** is divided into several groups. One is **Background Sources: Architecture and Design.** Another is **General Sources: American Furniture.** It includes publications for more than one region and is followed by alphabetized sources for the regions of the **Hawaiian Islands,** the **Mid-Atlantic,** the **Midwest, New England,** the **South,** the **Southwest,** and the **West.** Colonies or states are grouped in the traditional way according to the present name. References to Maryland and upstate New York remain, for example, under the Mid-Atlantic region, even though Maryland drew closer to the South in the nineteenth century and upstate New York often differs from the interests of New York City.

Periodicals

American Furniture, 1993–
The only publication devoted exclusively to American Furniture of all regions and periods; the annual should be consulted first for general inquiries; articles especially pertinent to furniture in this handbook are listed seperately.

The American Art Journal, 1969–

Antiques, 1922–

Antiques World, 1978–1982

Arts and Antiques, 1978–

Furniture History, 1965–

The Journal of the Classical Chinese Furniture Society, 1990–1994

The Journal of Decorative and Propaganda Arts, 1875–1945, 1986–

The Journal of Design History [England], 1988–

The Journal of Early Southern Decorative Arts, 1975–

Nineteenth Century, 1975–

Regional Furniture [England], 1987–

Studies in the Decorative Arts, 1993–

Victoria and Albert Museum Yearbook, One (1969)– Four (1973)

Winterthur Portfolio, I (1964)–

Books, Articles, and Manuscripts

BACKGROUND SOURCES: Architecture and Design

Adam, Peter. *Eileen Gray: Architect/Designer.* New York: Harry N. Abrams, Inc., 1987. Includes catalogue raisonné for Gray (1878–1976).

Agius, Pauline. *British Furniture: 1880–1915.* Woodbridge, Suffolk, England: Baron Publishing for the Antique Collectors' Club, 1978. Well-illustrated survey of mass-produced and custom-designed furniture.

Aldrich, Megan. *The Craces: Royal Decorators 1768–1899.* Introduction by Richard Marks. Brighton, England: The Royal Pavilion, Art Gallery, and Museum, 1990. Illustrated; unique insight into organization and operation of a prominent firm; it included furniture shops that produced designs by A. W. N. Pugin and other prominent designers.

———. *Gothic Revival.* London: Phaidon Press, Ltd., 1994. Subject confined to Great Britain; furniture included with other decorative arts, though emphasis on nineteenth-century architecture; excellent and numerous color illustrations of furniture in interiors not recorded elsewhere; selective bibliography.

Ames, Kenneth. "The Battle of the Sideboards." In *Winterthur Portfolio* 9 (1974): 1–27. French, English, and American sideboards exhibited 1851–1876 in international fairs are illustrated and analyzed as the major contemporary prestige furniture form; impact of design movements analyzed; they include Naturalistic, Renaissance, Rococo Revival, Adamesque, Louix XVI, Neo-Grec, and Reformed Gothic.

Antique Collectors' Club. *Pictorial Dictionary of British 19th-Century Furniture Design*. Introduction by Edward Joy. Woodbridge, Suffolk, England: Baron Publishing for the Antique Collectors' Club, 1977. Illustrations from nineteenth-century design books, price guides, and catalogues grouped by form and the identified sources discussed in the excellent introduction; the publication is an essential reference for the English background of nineteenth-century furniture.

Aslin, Elizabeth. *The Aesthetic Movement, Prelude to Art Nouveau*. New York: Frederick A. Praeger, 1969. Essential reference for the English background of American Art Furniture in the 1870s and 1880s.

———. *E. W. Godwin: Furniture and Interior Decoration*. London: John Murray, 1986. Authoritative study of a major force in the English Aesthetic Movement, which influenced American furniture in the 1870s and 1880s.

———. *Nineteenth Century English Furniture*. London: Faber, 1962. Excellent concise review of styles.

Atterbury, Paul, et al. *A. W. N. Pugin: Master of Gothic Revival*. New York: Yale University Press for Bard Graduate Center for Studies in the Decorative Arts, 1995. Catalogue for an exhibition at the Center in 1996.

———, and Wainwright, Clive, editors. *Pugin: A Gothic Passion*. New Haven and London: Yale University Press in association with the Victoria and Albert Museum, 1994. Catalogue for an exhibition at the Museum in 1994. See especially Wainwright "Furniture" but other essays pertinent for both decorative and reform movements in furniture.

Beard, Geoffrey, and Gilbert, Christopher, editors. *Dictionary of English Furniture Makers, 1660–1840*. London: Furniture History Society, 1986. Includes bibliography.

———. *Upholsterers & Interior Furnishing in England 1530–1840*. New Haven: Yale University Press in association with the Bard Graduate Center for Studies in the Decorative Arts, 1997.

Beyer, Victor; Hiesinger, Kathryn B.; Moulin, Jean-Marie; and Rishel, Joseph; exhibition organizers for the Philadelphia Museum of Art, The Detroit Institute of Arts, and the Musée du Louvre. *The Second Empire, 1852–1870: Art in France under Napoleon III*. Philadelphia: The Philadelphia Museum of Art, 1978. Catalogue for an exhibition at the museums in 1978–1979. See especially entries by the various authors for "Interior Views," pages 77–82, and "Furniture," pages 94–114; detailed and accurate information unavailable elsewhere that is pertinent for analysis of contemporary American styles.

Blumenson, John J.-G. *Indentifying American Architecture: A Pictorial Guide to Styles and Terms, 1600–1945*. Nashville, Tennessee: American Association of State and Local History, 1977. Introduction to architectural styles comparable to this guide for furniture; includes glossary of classical and other architectural motifs often adapted to furniture.

Brandt, Frederick R. *Late-19th and Early 20th-Century Decorative Arts: The Sydney and Frances Lewis Collection in the Virginia Museum of Fine Arts*. Richmond: The Virginia Museum of Fine Arts, 1985. Excellent collection stressing European furniture but including a few American examples; the collection and text are especially infor-mative for the background of American furniture of the 1920s and 1930s.

Brunhammer, Yvonne. *The Art Deco Style*. London: Academy Editions, 1983. Surveys European movement only.

Camard, Florence. *Ruhlman: Master of Art Deco*. Translated from French by David Macey. New York: Harry N. Abrams, Inc., 1984. Interiors, particularly furniture, by the designer (1879–1933), a significant French presence influential in the United States; illustrations, many in color, of furniture, contemporary photographs, and design sketches.

Chinnery, Victor. *Oak Furniture: The British Tradition: A History of Early Furniture in the British Isles and New England*. Woodbridge, Suffolk, England: Baron Publishing for the Antique Collectors' Club, 1979. Reprinted 1984; reprinted 1986 with additional pictorial index. New England furniture briefly discussed and date or orgin should be verified, but the context with British sixteenth- and seventeenth-century furniture is in-formative.

Collard, Frances. "Furniture." In *William Morris*. Linda Parry, editor. London: Philip Wilson Publishers in Association with The Victoria and Albert Museum, 1996. Published for an exhibition about Morris at the Museum in 1996. Analysis of furniture sold by firms with which Morris was associated.

Collins, Michael, and Papadakis, Andreas. *Post-Modern Design*. New York: Rizzoli International, 1989. Focus on international architects designing for manufacturers; Robert Venturi discussed Chapter IV, pages 103–121.

Cotton, Bernard D. *The English Regional Chair*. Woodbury, Suffolk, England: Antique Collectors' Club, 1990. Emphasis on Windsors; craftsman checklist; bibliography.

Crook, J. Mordaunt. *William Burges and the High Victorian Dream*. The University of Chicago Press, 1981. Furniture designs discussed as well as other decorative arts and architecture; analysis of Burges' place in the English Gothic Revival.

Curl, James Stevens. *The Egyptian Revival: An Introductory Study of a Recurring Theme in the History of Taste*. London: George Allen and Unwin, 1982. British and European architectural emphasis from Roman Empire to early twentieth century, but furniture included; bibliography; for the movement, see also this section Humbert, Jean-Marcel, et al. and *General Sources: American Furniture*, Bloemink, Barbara, et al.

Duncan, Alastair. *Art Nouveau Furniture*. New York: Clarkson N. Potter, Inc., 1982. International survey except for United States; bibliography for designers; excellent illustrations, some in color.

———. *Louis Majorelle: Master of Art Nouveau Design*. New York: Harry N. Abrams, Inc., 1991. Furniture emphasis; spare documentation; bibliography; excellent color illustrations.

Eames, Penelope. *Furniture in England, France, and the Netherlands from the Twelfth to the Fifteenth Century*. Leeds: The Furniture History Society, 1977. Published as volume XIII of *Furniture History*, the journal of the Furniture History Society. Authoritative and documented study of the use and appearance of furniture by type; illustrated by line drawings and photographic illustrations; excellent bibliography.

Edwards, Clive D. *Victorian Furniture: Technology and Design*. Manchester, England, and New York: Manchester University Press, 1993. Best available source for place of machine in British furniture industry; comparisons made with American furniture industry; traces gradual shift from craft to industry.

Ellsworth, Robert Hatfield. *Chinese Furniture: Hardwood Examples of the Ming and Early Ch'ing Dynasties*. New York: Random House, 1971. Authoritative presentation of stylistic and technical information.

Erikson, Svend. *Early Neo-Classicism in France*. Translated from French by Peter Thornton. London: Faber and Faber, 1974. Traces gradual replacement of Rococo by Neoclassicism 1750–1770; excellent and profuse illustrations, many in color, of furniture with other decorative arts.

Fiell, Charlotte and Peter. *Modern Furniture Classics since 1945*. Washington, D.C.: The American Institute of Architects Press, 1988. Appendices on museums, dealers, and designer biographies.

Garner, Philippe. *Twentieth-Century Furniture*. New York: Van Nostrand Reinhold Co., 1980. Innovative themes and designers among British, Europeans, and Americans analyzed by decades in a well-illustrated survey.

Gere, Charlotte. *Nineteenth-Century Decoration: The Art of the Interior*. New York: Harry N. Abrams, Inc., 1989. Essays and contemporary pictorial documentation, often in color, of town houses, country houses, cottages, and conservatories in Europe, Great Britain, India, and the United States; informative not only for style in furniture and upholstery, but also furniture use.

———, and Whiteway, Michael. *Nineteenth-Century Design: From Pugin to Mackintosh*. New York: Harry N. Abrams, Inc., 1994. Published in Great Britain in 1993 by George Weidenfeld and Nicolson Ltd. Essential background for American furniture reform movements; includes architecture and decorative arts other than furniture; appendix listing architects, designers, and manufacturers; selective bibliography, excellent illustrations, many in color.

Gilbert, Christopher. *The Life and Works of Thomas Chippendale*, 2 volumes. London: Studio Vista, in association with Christie, Manson & Woods Ltd., 1978. Documented and illustrated study with chapter about *The Gentleman and Cabinet-Maker's Director* (volume I, chapter 4, pages 65–107) and useful discussions of shop operation; letters, bills, and other documentation for furniture offer further insights into styles of the period.

———. *English Vernacular Furniture 1750–1900*. New Haven and London: Published for the Paul Mellon Centre for Studies in British Art by Yale University Press, 1991.

Gillow Archives, 1731–1932 [101 microfilm reels], 1971. These unique records of a major English furniture firm minutely document styles over two centuries. The Art Institute of Chicago and the Winterthur Museum are two libraries in the United States with a microfilm of the records in London at the City of Westminster Libraries, Archives Section.

Grandjean, Serge. *Empire Furniture: 1800 to 1825*. Taplinger Publishing Co., Inc., 1966. Concise, carefully researched, securely documented, and extensively illustrated survey of France only.

Hardy, John. "Rococo Furniture and Carving." In *Rococo Art and Design in Hogarth's England,* pages 153–188. London: The Victoria and Albert Museum, 1984. Catalogue for an exhibition at the museum in 1984. The publication generally and Hardy's contribution specifically are essential background for American furniture from the 1740s to the 1780s.

Harvey, Charles, and Press, John. *William Morris: Design and Enterprise in Victorian Britain.* Manchester, England: Manchester University Press, 1991. Discussion of economics and finances of Morris' firms proves that he emphasized profits and even turned to machines for increasing them, despite publicly endorsing handcraftsmanship; essential for study of American Arts and Crafts Movement.

Hayward, Helena, editor. *Thomas Johnson and English Rococo.* London: Alec Tiranti, 1964. Reprint of the then known published designs of the London carver printed from 1755 to 1762 and two known drawings; introductory essay places Johnson in eighteenth-century taste; sources listed and evaluated.

———, and Kirkham, Pat. *William and John Linnell: Eighteenth-Century London Furniture Makers.* New York: Rizzoli in association with Christie's, 1980. 2 volumes. Design process, management, workshop procedures, and patron relationships offer an insight into cabinetmaking elsewhere; appendices include glossary of terms and quotation of bills and correspondence; excellent bibliography.

Heskett, John. *German Design, 1870–1918.* New York: Taplinger Publishing Co., 1986. Furniture included in survey of concepts, designers, and artifacts; background for development of Bauhaus and American furniture 1930s to present.

Hiesinger, Kathryn B., and Marcus, George H. *Landmarks of Twentieth-Century Design: An Illustrated Handbook.* New York: Abbeville Press, 1993. Furniture included among 400 artifacts international in origin; appendix of designer biographies.

Himmelheber, Georg. *Biedermeir Furniture.* Translated and edited by Simon Jervis. London: Faber and Faber, 1974. Authoritative; period of furniture defined as circa 1814–1815 to circa 1848–1849; bibliography.

Horn, Richard. *Memphis: Objects, Furniture, and Patterns.* Second revised edition. Philadelphia: Running Press, 1986.

Humbert, Jean-Marcel; Pantazzi Michael; and Ziegler, Christianne. *Egyptomania: Egypt in Western Art, 1730–1930.* Ottawa: National Gallery of Canada, 1994. Catalogue for an exhibition at the Gallery, the Louvre, and the Kunsthistorisches in 1994–1995. Furniture included in emphasis on British and European arts; for the movement, see also this section Curl, James Stevens and *General Sources: American Furniture,* Bloemink, Barbara, et al.

Joy, Edward. *Pictorial Dictionary of British 19th-Century Furniture Design.* Woodbridge, Suffolk, England: The Antique Collectors' Club, 1977. About 5,000 designs from 49 design books organized by form or function; informative introductory essay entitled "The Designers and Design Books."

Kinmouth, Claudia. *Irish Country Furniture 1700–1950.* New Haven: Yale University Press, 1993. Thorough, well-documented, well-illustrated (often in color) survey based on surviving furniture and contemporary pictorial sources; checklist of pertinent museum collections; glossary of terms; gazeteer; bibliographic note.

Kirkham, Pat. "Living Fancy: Mackintosh Furniture and Interiors." In *Charles Rennie Mackintosh,* pages 227–262. Wendy Kaplan, editor. New York: Abbeville Press for Glasgow Museums, 1996. Catalogue for an exhibition organized by Glasgow Museums, Glasgow School of Art, and the Hunterian Museum and Art Gallery, University of Glasgow, The Metropolitan Museum of Art, The Art Institute of Chicago, and the Los Angeles County Museum of Art, 1996–1997. Other essays and illustrations refer to furniture.

Knell, David. *English Country Furniture: The National & Regional Vernacular 1500–1900.* New York: Cross River Press, 1992. Despite title, includes furniture in "everyday" use, whether urban or rural.

Lever, Jill. *Architects' Designs for Furniture.* New York: Rizzoli International Publications, Inc., 1982. Furniture designs from the late-16th century to the early-20th in the collection of The Royal Institute of British Architects (London). Informative essays about each architect's furniture interest and his contribution to stylistic movements.

McFadden, David Revere. Exhibition administrator for the Cooper-Hewitt Museum, New York City, and the Carnegie Museum of Art, Pittsburgh. *Courts and Colonies: The William and Mary Style in Holland, England, and America.* Seattle and London: University of Washington Press, 1988. Essays and catalogue entries by various authors; essential reference for the style.

Macquoid, Percy, and Edwards, Ralph. *The Dictionary of English Furniture from the Middle Ages to the Late Georgian Period.* 3 volumes. Second revised edition by Ralph Edwards. London: County Life, 1954. Illustrated survey of sophisticated and vernacular furniture with reliable term definitions.

Mang, Karl. *History of Modern Furniture.* Translated by John Williams Gabriel. New York: Harry N. Abrams, Inc., 1979. European and American innovative concepts in design and fabrication traced from the 1840s to the 1970s.

Massey, Anne. *Interior Design of the 20th Century.* New York: Thames and Hudson Ltd., 1990. Includes American, British, European furniture in interiors; perceptive discussion of styles; informative illustrations from contemporary photographs not available elsewhere; selective bibliography.

Morley, John. *Regency Designs, 1790–1840.* New York: Harry N. Abrams, Inc., 1993. See especially "Furniture" (Part IV), pages 354–427; furniture illustrated elsewhere in text; the most authoritative analysis of the diverse Classical, Gothic, Chinese, and other revivals in the period, which the author extends beyond the political regency of George, Prince of Wales, from 1811 to 1820.

Mowl, Timothy. *Elizabethan and Jacobean Style.* London: Phaidon Press, 1993.

Ostergard, Derek D., et al. *Bent Wood and Metal Furniture: 1850–1946.* New York: The University of Washington Press in association with the American Federation of the Arts, 1987. Catalogue for an exhibition of European and American furniture circulated 1986–1988; glossary; bibliography.

Palardy, Jean. *The Early Furniture of French Canada.* Translated from French by Eric McLean. Toronto and New York: Macmillan of Canada and St. Martins Press, 1965. Includes 17th-, 18th-, and 19-century furniture in collections of Canada and the United States.

Pallot, Bill G. B. *The Art of the Chair in Eighteenth-Century France.* Foreword by Theodore Dell. Preface by Svend Erickson. Paris: ACR-Gesmondi, Courbevoie, 1989.

Parissien, Steven. *Adam Style.* Washington, D.C.: The Preservation Press of the National Trust for Historic Preservation, 1992. See especially Chapter Six, pages 183–211, "Furniture": author traces design changes over Robert Adam's career and his influence on English contemporaries; Adam's American influence suggested; excellent illustrations, often in color, include drawings, pictures, and prints; text not documented; "Further Reading" serves as selective biography.

Payne, Christopher. *19th-Century European Furniture.* Woodbridge, Suffolk, England: Antique Collectors' Club, Reprint in 1989 of 2nd edition in 1985. Compendium of photographs with commentaries by form, function, and occasionally decoration; includes comments on materials; bibliography.

Pradere, Alexandre. *French Furniture Makers: The Art of the Ébéniste from Louis XIV to the Revolution.* Translated from French by Perran Wood. Malibu, California: The J. Paul Getty Museum, 1989. Glossary of French terms, woods, list of makers; bibliography.

Sekler, Eduard Franz. *Josef Hoffman: The Architectural Work.* Translated from German by the author and John Maas. Princeton, New Jersey: Princeton University Press, 1985. Record of furniture designed by Hoffman (1870–1956) in room views in architectural catalogue raisonné; photographs often contemporary with buildings now destroyed or furnishings dispersed.

Shixiang, Wang. *Classic Chinese Furniture: Ming and Early Qing Dynasties.* Translated by Sarah Handler and the author. London: Han-Shan Tang Ltd., 1986. A catalogue of 175 objects in China includes color photographs (usually with details) and a commentary introduced by essays about woods, construction, and use.

Smith, Thomas Gordon. *Neo-Classical Furniture Designs: A Reprint of Thomas King's "Modern Style of Cabinet Work Exemplified", 1829.* New York: Dover Publications, 1995. Includes King's biography, his influence in England and the United States, and a list of King's design books.

Stillman, Damie. *The Decorative Work of Robert Adam.* New York: Transatlantic Arts, 1966. Emphasis on interior architecture and standing furniture designed as an integral part of wall compositions; other furniture not discussed.

Thornton, Peter. *Seventeenth-Century Interior Decoration in England, France and Holland.* New Haven and London: Yale University Press for the Paul Mellon Centre for Studies in British Art, 1978. Authoritative and well illustrated; chapters on beds (VII), upholstered seat furniture (VIII), tables and cupboards (IX), and such miscellaneous forms as screens, looking glasses, and ornamental cabinets (X).

———. *Authentic Decor: The Domestic Interior, 1620–1920.* London: Weidenfeld and Nicolson, 1984. Seven periods documented by 532 carefully selected contemporary paintings, water colors, prints, and drawings with an essay for each; includes northern Europe, Great Britain, Scandinavia, and the United States; documents and dates sophisticated and vernacular furniture.

———. *The Italian Renaissance Interior, 1400–1600.* New York: Harry N. Abrams, Inc., 1991. Text discusses contemporary pictorial sources, most with furniture: see especially "Part Two," pages 111–261, for furniture by form; excellent illustrations, many in color; thorough documentation.

Toher, Jennifer. "Furniture and Interior Decoration." In *Encyclopedia of Art Deco*, Alastair Duncan, editor. New York: E. P. Dutton, 1988. Survey of varied movements, including those in the United States.

Tomlin, Maurice. *Catalogue of Adam Period Furniture.* London: Victoria and Albert Museum, 1982. English furniture; entirely or partly Neo-Classical designed by Robert Adam's firm and others dating 1760–1800; essay about each object includes illustrations of designs, materials, measurements, and provenance; confined to collection of Victoria and Albert Museum; excellent bibliography.

Troy, Nancy. *Modernism and the Decorative Arts in France: Art Nouveau to Le Corbusier.* New Haven: Yale University Press, 1991. Comprehensive bibliography.

Watkins, David. *Thomas Hope, 1769–1831, and the Neo-Classical Idea.* London: John Murry, 1968. See especially Chapter VII, "The Hope Style: Sources, Parallels, and Influences."

Weisberg, Gabriel P. *Art Nouveau Bing: Paris Style 1900.* New York: Harry N. Abrams, Inc., in association with the Smithsonian Institution Traveling Exhibitions Service (SITES), 1986. Background of the shop, designers, workshops, and furniture sold (among other objects); authoritative analysis; excellent bibliography; essential background for American furniture 1896–1914.

White, Elizabeth. *Pictorial Dictionary of British 18th Century Furniture Design: The Printed Sources.* Woodbridge, Suffolk, England: Antique Collectors' Club Ltd., 1990. About 3,000 designs illustrated and organized by form or function with introductory essays; informative "Notes on the Designers"; selective bibliography; supplements Peter Ward-Jackson, *English Furniture Designs of the Eighteenth Century* (London: Her Majesty's Stationery Office, 1958).

Wilk, Christopher, et al. *Western Furniture: 1350 to the Present Day in the Victoria and Albert Museum, London.* New York: Cross River Press, 1996. Essays for about 100 examples, including American, with illustrations of objects, often in color, and related objects; excellent documentation and technical information; documents No. 89 in this pictoral guide.

GENERAL SOURCES: American Furniture

Adamson, Jeremy. *American Wicker: Woven Furniture from 1850 to 1930.* Washington, D. C.: The Renwick Gallery of the National Museum of American Art, Smithsonian Institution, in association with Rizzoli, 1993. Catalogue for an exhibition at the Gallery in 1993. Comprehensive; reliable; secure documentation; many illustrations, frequently in color; selective bibliography.

Ames, Kenneth L. "What is neo-grec?" and "Sitting in (Neo-Grec) Style." *Nineteenth Century* 2, nos. 2, 3–4 (Summer, Autumn 1976): pages 13–21, 51–58.

Barquist, David L., with essays by Elizabeth Donaghy Garrett and Gerald W. R. Ward. *American Tables and Looking Glasses in the Mabel Brady Garvan and Other Collections at Yale University.* New Haven: Yale University Art Gallery, 1992.; Documentation for No. 60 in this book.

Bloemink, Barbara, et al. *The Sphinx and the Lotus: The Egyptian Movement in American Decorative Arts, 1865–1935.* Yonkers, New York: The Hudson River Museum, 1990. Catalogue for an exhibition at the Museum, 1990. Furniture included with other decorative arts; for European movement see Curl, James Stevens and Humbert, Jean-Marcel in *Background Sources: Architecture and Design.*

Cooke, Edward S. *New American Furniture.* Boston: The Museum of Fine Arts, 1989. Discussion of twenty-five artisans the author considers in the second generation of "studio makers"; metal, plastic, and wicker furniture not included.

———, editor. *Upholstery in America and Europe from the Seventeenth Century to World War I.* New York and London: W. W. Norton and Co., for the Barra Foundation, 1987. Twenty illustrated and well-documented articles by Cooke and others; contents are not as inclusive as the title states.

———. "Arts and Crafts Furniture: Process or Product?" in *The Ideal Home, 1900–1920: The History of Twentieth-Century American Craft*, pages 64–76. New York: Harry N. Abrams in association with the American Craft Museum, 1993. Catalogue for an exhibition at the Museum, 1993. The most authoritative discussion of Arts and Crafts wooden furniture; metal and wicker furniture not included.

Cooper, Wendy A. *Classical Taste in America 1800–1840.* New York: The Baltimore Museum of Art and Abbeville Press, 1993. Catalogue for an exhibition at the Museum, The Mint Museum of Art, Charlotte, North Carolina, and The Museum of Fine Arts, Houston, 1993–1994. Furniture included with painting, sculpture, and other decorative arts; bibliography.

Davies, Karen. *At Home in Manhattan: Modern Decorative Arts, 1925 to the Depression.* New Haven: Yale University Art Gallery, 1983. Furniture included in a documented and illustrated survey.

Dietz, Ulysses G. *Century of Revivals: Nineteenth-Century American Furniture from the Collection of the Newark Museum.* Newark, New Jersey: The Museum, 1982.

Domergue, Denise. *Artists Design Furniture.* New York: Harry N. Abrams, Inc., 1984. Furniture designed by sixty-seven artists since World War II with their comments about their approaches.

Dubrow, Eileen and Richard. *American Furniture of the 19th Century, 1840–1880.* Exton, Pennsylvania: Schiffer Publications, 1983.

Duncan, Alastair. *American Art Deco.* New York: Harry N. Abrams, Inc., 1986. The chapter on furniture, pages 31–65, includes commissioned and mass-produced objects.

Elder, William Voss, II, and Stokes, Jane E., et al. *American Furniture 1680–1880,* from the Collection of the Baltimore Museum of Art. Baltimore, Maryland: Baltimore Museum of Art, 1987.

Evans, Nancy Goyne. *American Windsor Chairs.* New York: Hudson Hills Press in association with The Henry Francis du Pont Winterthur Museum, 1996. Authoritative survey.

———. *American Windsor Furniture: Specialized Forms.* New York, New York: The Winterthur Museum in association with Hudson Hills Press, 1997.

Fales, Dean A. *American Painted Furniture.* New York: Dutton, 1972. Excellent pictorial record; attributions and dates should be verified in subsequent publications; bibliography.

Flanigan, J. Michael, with introductory essays by Wendy A. Cooper, Morrison H. Heckscher, and Gregory R. Weidman. *American Furniture from the Kauffman Collection.* Washington: The National Gallery of Art, 1986. Color illustrations, technical notes, and commentaries for 101 objects collected by Mr. and Mrs. George Kauffman; emphasis on the late-18th and early-19th centuries.

Forman, Benno M. *American Seating Furniture, 1630–1730: An Interpretive Catalogue.* Winterthur, Delaware: W. W. Norton & Co., for the Winterthur Museum. Catalogue of the Winterthur collection.

Hanks, David A., with essays by Rodris Roth and Page Talbot. *Innovative Furniture in America: From 1880 to the Present.* New York: Horizon Press,1981. Includes bibliography.

———, with Jenifer Toher and an essay by Jeffrey L. Meikle. *Donald Deskey: Decorative Designs and Interiors.* New York: E. P. Dutton, 1987. Life and work of a major designer from the 1920s to the 1950s.

———, and Peirce, Donald C. *The Virginia Carroll Crawford Collection: American Decorative Arts, 1825–1917.* Atlanta, Georgia: The High Museum of Art, 1983. Includes furniture with brief comments on objects.

Heckscher, Morrison H. *American Furniture in the Metropolitan Museum of Art: Late Colonial Period, The Queen Anne and Chippendale Periods.* New York: The Museum and Random House, 1985. Concise technical notes and excellent illustrations for 213 objects.

———. "Philadelphia Chippendale: The Influence of the *Director* in America," *Furniture History* XXI (1985), pages 283–288, figures 1–23.

———, and Bowman, Leslie Green. *American Rococo, 1750–1775: Elegance in Ornament.* New York: The Metropolitan Museum of Art and the Los Angeles County Museum of Art, 1992. Catalogue for an exhibition at the museums, 1992–1993. Furniture included with other decorative arts and architectural decoration; the most comprehensive study of the subject.

Herman, Lloyd E., with research by Dezso Sekely. *A Modern Consciousness: D. J. De Pree, Florence Knoll.* Washington D.C.: Smithsonian Institute for the National Collection of Fine Arts, 1975. Careers of two people significant in two major firms in post World War II furniture, Herman Miller, Inc., and Knoll International.

Hewitt, Benjamin A.; Kane, Patricia E.; and Ward, Gerald W. R. *The Work of Many Hands: Card Tables in Federal America, 1790–1820.* New Haven: The Yale University Art Gallery, 1982. Analysis of card tables for local and regional features.

Hiesinger, Kathryn B., and Marcus, George H., editors. *Design Since 1945.* Philadelphia: The Philadelphia Museum of Art, 1983. Furniture by Americans included in an illustrated international survey with essays by designers and biographies of them; bibliographies included for the designers and concepts.

Howe, Katherine S., and Warren, David B., with introduction by Jane B. Davies. *The Gothic-Revival Style in America, 1830–1870.* Houston: The Museum of Fine Arts, Houston, 1976. Unique and authoritative study.

Hummel, Charles F. *A Winterthur Guide to American Chippendale Furniture: Middle Atlantic and Southern Colonies.* New York: Crown Publishers for Rutledge Books, 1976.

Israel Sack, Inc. *Opportunities in American Antiques.* New York: Israel Sack, Inc., 1957– . Occasional brochures with illustrations and comments about furniture for sale; objects date from the 17th, 18th, and early 19th centuries. Brochures collected and republished in book form as *American Antiques from Israel Sack Collection.* Washington D. C.: Highland House Publishers, Inc., vol. I (1969)– .

Johnson, Marilynn "The Artful Interior" and "Art Furniture: Wedding the Beautiful to the Useful." In *In Pursuit of Beauty: Americans and the Aesthetic Movement,* pages 110–175. Catalogue for an exhibition at the Museum in 1986. New York: The Metropolitan Museum of Art and Rizzoli International Publications, 1986.

Johnston, Phillip M. "The William and Mary Style in America." In *Courts and Colonies: The William and Mary Style in Holland, England, and America,* pages 62–79, and pertinent catalogue entries. Seattle and London: University of Washington Press, 1988. Essential reference for evolution of style in America.

Kane, Patricia E. *300 Years of Seating Furniture: Chairs and Beds from the Mabel Brady Garvan and Other Collections at Yale University.* Boston: The New York Graphic Society, 1976. Documentation for No. 196 in this book.

Kaplan, Wendy, editor. *"The Art that is Life": The Arts & Crafts Movement in America, 1875–1920.* Boston: The Museum of Fine Arts, 1987. Furniture included in essays as a facet of the movement.

Kirk, John T. *American Furniture & the British Tradition to 1830.* New York: Knopf, with distribution by Random House, 1982.

Levy, Bernard and S. Dean. *An American Tea Party: An Exhibition of Colonial Tea and Breakfast Tables, 1715–1783.* New York: Bernard & S. Dean Levy, Inc., 1988. Thirty-eight examples from public and private collections.

Madigan, Mary Jean Smith. "The Influence of Charles Locke Eastlake on American Furniture Manufacture, 1870–90." *Winterthur Portfolio* 10 (1975): 1–22.

Monkhouse, Christopher P., and Michie, Thomas S., with the assistance of John M. Carpenter. *American Furniture in Pendleton House.* Providence, Rhode Island: Rhode Island School of Design, 1986. Illustrations, technical notes, and essays for 164 objects dating from the 17th century to the present in a house built as a setting for the collection; excellent bibliography.

Montgomery, Charles F. *American Furniture: The Federal Period in the Henry Francis du Pont Winterthur Museum.* New York: Viking Press, 1966. Excellent technical and pictorial record; attributions should be verified by subsequent publications.

Naeve, Milo M. *The Classical Presence in American Art.* Chicago: The Art Institute of Chicago, 1978. Illustrated essay about Greek and Roman influences on American art, including furniture, from the 17th to the 20th centuries.

———. "American Arts: Furniture." In *A Decade of Decorative Arts: The Antiquarian Society of the Art Institute of Chicago.* Chicago: The Art Institute of Chicago, 1986. Essays on twelve 18th- and 19th-century objects given by the Society to the Art Institute. In this study, the objects include Nos. 18, 21, 25, 39, 118, 120.

Neuhart, John; Neuhart, Marilyn; and Eames, Ray. *Eames Design: The Work of the Office of Charles and Ray Eames.* New York: Harry N. Abrams, Inc., 1989. Furniture included chronologically with all projects; definitive and authoritative compilation by designer's wife and staff;

staff design participants, once obscured by firm, cited for each project; documentation for nos. 142 and 144 in this book.

Nordness, Lee. *Objects USA.* New York: A Studio Book, Viking Press, 1970. Survey of crafts at the time of publication through innovative objects; biographies of craftsmen.

Phillips, Lisa. *Shape and Environment: Furniture by American Architects.* New York: The Whitney Museum of American Art, Fairfield County, 1982. General bibliography and bibliographies for each architect included.

———. *High Styles: Twentieth-Century Design.* New York: The Whitney Museum of American Art, in association with Summit Books, 1985. Essays by Phillips and others analyzing eclectic and innovative styles.

Pilgrim, Diane H. "The Decorative Art: The Domestic Environment." In *The American Renaissance: 1876–1917,* pages 110–151. Brooklyn: The Brooklyn Museum, 1979.

———. "Design for the Machine." In *The Machine Age in America, 1918–1941,* pages 271–337. New York: The Brooklyn Museum in association with Harry N. Abrams, Inc., 1986. Emphasis on mass-production with comment on furniture.

Rieman, Timothy D., and Burks, Jean M. *The Complete Book of Shaker Furniture.* New York: Harry N. Abrams, Inc., 1993. The most comprehensive study of the subject; secure documentation includes extensive quotation from primary sources; excellent illustrations, many in color; selective bibliography.

Sack, Albert. *The New Fine Points of Furniture: Early American.* New York: Crown Publishers, Inc., 1993. Unique study of quality in American furniture emphasizing objects before 1820.

Semowich, Charles J. *American Furniture Craftsman Working Prior to 1920: An Annotated Bibliography.* Westport, Connecticut, and London, England: Greenwood Press, 1984. Includes lists of pertinent trade catalogues, furniture periodicals, and manuscript collections.

Smith, Paul J. *New Handmade Furniture: American Furniture Makers Working in Hardwood.* New York: The American Craft Museum, 1979. Includes Stewart Paul, Lee M. Rohde, Lee A. Schuette, Alan Siegel, John Snedicor, Michael Speaker, and Daniel Loomis Valenza.

———, with introductory essay about American crafts since the 1890s by Edward Lucie-Smith. *Craft Today: Poetry of the Physical.* New York: The American Craft Museum, 1986. Includes furniture with other objects, excellent chronology of events and major exhibitions in American crafts from 1851–1986, detailed biographies of craftsmen, general bibliography, and a limited bibliography for furniture under the category "Wood."

Stein, Susan R. *The Worlds of Thomas Jefferson at Monticello.* Harry N. Abrams, Inc. in association with the Thomas Jefferson Memorial Foundation, Inc., 1993. Section on "Furniture" discusses 56 examples, mostly American, with Monticello associations.

Stephenson, Sue H. *Rustic Furniture.* New York: Van Nostrand Rheinhold Company, 1979. Emphasis on 19th-century American versions with survey of European and Oriental background; includes techniques for making furniture.

Stone, Michael A. *Contemporary American Woodworkers.* Salt Lake City: Gibbs M. Smith, Inc., 1986. Illustrated commentary about Wharton Esherick, George Nakashima, Bob Stocksdale, Tage Frid, Sam Maloof, Arthur Espenet Carpenter, James Krenov, Wendell Castle, Garry Knox Bennett, and Jere Osgood.

Teller, Betty. "American Furniture in the Art Nouveau Style." In *Art & Antiques* 3, no. 3 (May–June 1980): pages 96–101. Foremost publication on the subject.

Trent, Robert F. "The Chest of Drawers in America, 1635–1730: A Postscript." In *Winterthur Portfolio* 20 (1985): 31–48. Amplifies Forman, Benno M. "The Chest of Drawers in America, 1635–1730: The Origin of the Joined Chest of Drawers." In *Winterthur Portfolio* 20 (1985): 1–30. Traces evolution of chest of drawers in England and introduction to America; documentation for No. 15 in this book.

Venable, Charles L. *The Faith P. and Charles L. Bybee Collection of American Furniture.* Dallas, Texas: The Dallas Museum of Art, 1986. Collection includes 18th- and early 19th-centuries; technical notes; well documented; bibliography.

Voorsanger, Catherine Hoover. "Dictionary of Architects, Artisans, Artists, and Manufacturers." In *In Pursuit of Beauty: Americans and the Aesthetic Movement,* pages 401–487. New York: The Metropolitan Museum of Art and Rizzoli International Publications, 1986. Includes significant innovators in furniture design and fabrication with an excellent bibliography for each entry.

Ward, Gerald W. R. *American Case Furniture in the Mabel Brady Garvan and Other Collections at Yale University.* New Haven: The Yale University Art Gallery, 1988. Thorough comments with excellent illustrations. Documentation for No. 4 in this study.

Wilk, Christopher. *Marcel Breuer: Furniture and Interiors.* Introduction by J. Stewart Johnson. New York: The Museum of Modern Art, 1981. European and American careers treated separately with excellent illustrations and thorough documentation.

REGIONAL SOURCES: **Hawaiian Islands**

Hackler, Rhoda E. A. *Koa Furniture of Hawaii.* Honolulu: University of Hawaii Department of Art, Partners, and the Daughters of Hawaii, 1981. Includes bibliography.

Jenkins, Irving. *Hawaiian Furniture and Hawaii's Cabinetmakers, 1820–1941.* Honolulu: Editions Ltd., for the Daughters of Hawaii, 1983. Includes bibliography.

REGIONAL SOURCES: **Mid-Atlantic**

Ames, Kenneth L. "Designed in France: Notes on the Transmission of French Style to America." In *Winterthur Portfolio* 12 (1977): 103–114. George Henkels, a major Philadelphia cabinetmaker of the 1850s and 1860s, documented as importing French furniture, books, and journals as design exemplars.

Blackburn, Roderic H., and Piwanka, Ruth, et al. *Remembrance of Patria: Dutch Arts and Culture in Colonial America, 1609–1776.* Albany, New York: Albany Institute of History and Art, 1988. Furniture included with fine arts and other decorative arts; bibliography.

Butler, Joseph T. *Sleepy Hollow Restorations: A Cross-Section of the Collection.* Tarrytown, New York: Sleepy Hollow Restorations, 1983. Includes furniture; excellent technical notes.

D'Ambrosio, Anna Tobin. *The Distinction of Being Different: Joseph P. McHugh and the American Arts and Crafts Movement.* Essay by Leslie Green Bowman on McHugh's place in the Arts and Crafts Movement. Utica, New York: Munson-Williams-Proctor Institute, 1993. The term "Mission Furniture" is persuasively traced in a well-documented text to McHugh between 1894 and 1897; he made and sold commercial versions of Arts and Crafts furniture in New York City; well illustrated; excellent furniture catalogue; excellent bibliography.

de Julio, Mary Antoine. *German Folk Arts of New York State.* Albany, New York: The Albany Institute of History and Art, 1985. Furniture included with other arts; authoritative illustrated commentary.

Dorman, Charles G. "Delaware Cabinetmakers and Allied Artisans, 1655–1855." In *Delaware History* 9 (1960): 111–217. See also this section, Hancock, Harold B.

Edwards, Robert and Aibel. *Robert Wharton Esherick, 1887–1970, American Woodworker.* Philadelphia: Modern Gallery, 1996. Catalogue for an exhibition of furniture for sale at the Gallery, 1996. Essay about Wharton and information about 41 objects, mostly furniture; background for Nos. 150 and 152 in this book.

Fabian, Monroe H. *The Pennsylvania-German Decorated Chest.* New York: Universe Books, 1978.

Failey, Dean F. *Long Island Is My Nation: The Decorative Arts and Craftsmen, 1640–1830.* Setauket, New York: The Society for the Preservation of Long Island Antiquities, 1977.

Garvan, Beatrice B. *Federal Philadelphia, 1785–1825: The Athens of the Western World.* Philadelphia: The Philadelphia Museum of Art, 1987. Furniture included with other arts and crafts.

———. *The Pennsylvania German Collection.* Philadelphia: The Philadelphia Museum of Art, 1982. Descriptive and technical notes for furniture in the illustrated section devoted to the medium of wood; the collection is the most comprehensive.

———, and Hummel, Charles F. editors. *The Pennsylvania Germans: A Celebration of Their Arts, 1683–1850.* The Philadelphia Museum of Art and the Henry Francis du Pont Winterthur Museum, 1982. Contributions by Garvan and Hummel with seven other specialists; furniture included in topical essays.

Gilborn, Craig. *Adirondack Furniture and the Rustic Tradition.* New York: Abrams, 1987. Furniture made in the Adirondack Park and imported from Indiana, Ohio, Pennsylvania, and Ontario from the 1880s to the 1920s.

Gray, Nina. "Leon Marcotte: Cabinetmaker and Interior Decorator." In *American Furniture 1994,* pages 49–72. Secure documentation for operation of major decorating firm, which typically owned furniture shops; a specialist in Louis XVI Style; background for armchair No. 90 in this book.

Griffith, Lee Ellen. *The Pennsylvania Spice Box: Paneled Doors and Secret Drawers.* West Chester, Pennsylvania: The Chester County Historical Society, 1986.

Hancock, Harold. B. "Furniture Craftsmen in Delaware Records." *Winterthur Portfolio* 9 (1974): pages 175–221. See also this section, Dorman, Charles G.

Harwood, Barry R. *The Furniture of George Hunzinger: Invention and Innovation in Nineteenth-Century America.* New York: The Brooklyn Museum of Art, 1997. In this book, documentation for No. 77.

Horner, William Macpherson, Jr. *Blue Book, Philadelphia Furniture: William Penn to George Washington with Special Reference to the Philadelphia Chippendale School.* Philadelphia: Privately Printed, 1935. Second printing with index and revised captions, Washington, D.C.: Highland House Publishers, Inc., 1977.

Howe, Katherine S.; Frelinghuysen, Alice Cooney; Voorsanger, Catherine Hoover. *Herter Brothers: Furniture and Interiors for a Gilded Age.* New York: Harry N. Abrams, Inc., in association with The Museum of Fine Arts, Houston, 1994. Catalogue for an exhibition at the Museum of Fine Arts, Houston, The Metropolitan Museum of Art, and High Museum of Art, Atlanta, 1994–1995. Among the securely documented essays, Voorsanger's "From the Bowery to Broadway: The Herter Brothers and the New York Furniture Trade," pages 56–77, is informative for cabinetmaking and decorating in New York City during the period; catalogue with color illustrations and technical notes for forty-two objects designed by the firm of Gustave and Christian Herter in New York City from 1858 to 1883.

Hummel, Charles F. *With Hammer in Hand: The Dominy Craftsmen of East Hampton, New York.* Charlottesville: University Press of Virginia for the Winterthur Museum, 1968. Furniture, tools, materials, and craft procedures of the Dominy family in the 18th and early 19th centuries offer an insight into practices elsewhere.

James, Michael L. *Drama in Design: The Life and Craft of Charles Rohlfs.* Buffalo: Burchfield Art Center, Buffalo State College, 1994. Published in connection with an exhibition at the Center entitled *The Craftsmanship of Charles Rohlfs in 1994.*

Kenny, Peter M.; Safford, Frances Gruber; and Vincent, Gilbert T. *American Kasten: The Dutch-Style Cupboards of New York and New Jersey, 1650–1800.* New York: The Metropolitan Museum of Art, 1991. Catalogue for an exhibition at the Museum in 1991. The definitive statement on the subject; document for No. 160 in this book.

———; Leben, Ulrich; and Bretter, Frances F. *Honoré Lannuier, Cabinet Maker from Paris: The Life and Work of a French Ébéniste in Federal New York.* New York: The Metropolitan Museum of Art, 1998. In this book, background for Nos. 56, 57, 58, 61.

Levy, Bernard and S. Dean. *"Opulence and Splendor"; The New York Chair, 1690–1830.* New York: Bernard & S. Dean Levy, Inc., 1984.

Levy, Frank M. "A Maker of New York Card Tables Identified." In *Antiques,* 143, no. 5 (May 1993); pages 756–763. Marinus Willet and Jonathan Pearsee identified as the makers of nine Chippendale examples; secure documentation. In this book, background for No. 30.

Lucie-Smith, Edward. *The Art of William Payley.* New York: Harry N. Abrams, Inc., 1996. "Furniture" discussed Chapter 4, pages 40-53; text not documented; excellent illustrations, some in color; includes selective "Catalogue of Works," list of museums where Paley represented, chronology, and selective bibliography. In this book, background for No. 154.

Naeve, Milo M. "An Aristocratic Windsor in Eighteenth-Century Philadelphia." *The American Art Journal* 11, no. 3 (July 1979): pages 66–74. Stylistic, technical, and cultural context of a walnut Windsor armchair, currently a unique survival; Walnut Windsors documented to Philadelphia; in this book, it is No. 195.

———. "Louis Comfort Tiffany and the Reform Movement in Furniture Design: The J. Matthew Meier and Ernest Hagen Commission of 1882–1885." In *American Furniture 1996,* pages 3–16. Milwaukee, Wisconsin: Chipstone Foundation, 1996. Documentation for Nos. 108 and 109 in this book.

Nakashima, George. *The Soul of a Tree: A Woodworker's Reflections.* Introduction by George Wald. Tokyo: Kodansha International Ltd., 1981. Autobiography of the craftsman who lived in New Hope, Pennsylvania; illustrations of furniture, chronology, awards, exhibitions, selected architectural commmsisions, bibliography, and glossary. Documentation for No. 199 in this book.

Ostergard, Derek E. *George Nakashima: Full Circle.* Introduction by Sam Maloof; essay by George Nakashima. New York: Weidenfeld & Nicholson, 1989. Survey of the craftsman's furniture. Documentation for No. 199 in this book.

Reed, Henry; Yoder, Don; and Fabian, Monroe. *Decorated Furniture of the Mahantongo Valley.* Philadelphia: University of Pennsylvania Press, 1987. Checklist and discussion of all recorded furniture with comment on craftsmen and decorators.

Rice, Norman S. *New York Furniture before 1840 in the Collection of the Albany Institute of History and Art.* Albany: The Albany Institute, 1962.

Scherer, John L. *New York Furniture at the New York State Museum.* Albany: Division of Historical Anthropological Services, The New York State Museum, The State Education Department, 1984. Furniture dates from 1680–1810, much of it documented by maker and owner.

———. *New York Furniture: The Federal Period 1788–1825.* Albany: University of the State of New York, 1988. Includes some entries from the author's 1984 publication with many recent accessions.

Schiffer, Margaret Berwind. *Furniture and Its Makers of Chester County, Pennsylvania.* Philadelphia: University of Pennsylvania Press, 1966. Includes craftsman checklist.

Schwartz, Marvin D.; Stanek, Edward; and True, Douglas. *The Furniture of John Henry Belter and the Rococo Revival.* New York: E. P. Dutton, 1981.

Sewell, Darrel, et al. *Philadelphia: Three Centuries of American Art.* Philadelphia: The Philadelphia Museum of Art, 1976. Furniture entries by Beatrice Garvan, David Hanks, and Page Talbott; the study ranges from 1676 to 1976.

Taragin, Daviras; Cooke, Edward S., Jr.; and Giovannini, Joseph. Foreword by Sachs, Samuel II. *Furniture by Wendell Castle.* New York: Hudson Hills Press in association with the Founders' Society, Detroit Institute of the Arts, 1989. Catalogue for an exhibition at the Institute; Delaware Art Museum, Wilmington; Virginia Museum of Fine Arts, Richmond; Memorial Art Gallery, University of Rochester, New York: and American Craft Museum, New York City, 1989–1991. Essays on aspects of the subject; catalogue for forty-nine objects; bibliography by year published; exhibition checklist.

Tracy, Berry B. *Federal Furniture and Decorative Arts at Boscobel.* New York: Boscobel Restoration, Inc., 1981. Furnishings of a restored house near New York City.

Wainwright, Nicholas B. *Colonial Grandeur in Philadelphia.* Foreword by Henry Francis du Pont. Philadelphia: The Historical Society of Pennsylvania, 1964. Documentation for furniture John Cadwalader commissioned 1769–1770 for one of the most lavish American town houses of the period.

Waters, Deborah Dependahl. *Plain and Ornamental: Delaware Furniture 1740–1890.* Introduction by Charles G. Dorman. Wilmington: The Historical Society of Delaware, 1984.

———. "Is It Phyfe?" In *American Furniture 1996,* pages 63–80. Characteristics of furniture by contemporaries of Duncan Phyfe (1768–1854) and later craftsmen adapting his Style.

Zimmerman, Philip D. and Levy, Frank M. "An important block-front desk by Richard Walker of Boston." In *Antiques,* 147, no. 3 (March 1995), 436–441. In this book, documentation for No. 29.

REGIONAL SOURCES: Midwest

Connell, E. Jane, and Muller, Charles R. *Made in Ohio: Furniture, 1788–1888.* Columbus: The Columbus Museum of Art, 1984. Includes bibliography.

Darling, Sharon S. *Chicago Furniture: 1833–1983.* New York: The Chicago Historical Society, in association with W. W. Norton, 1984. Includes bibliography.

Gray, Stephen, editor. *Arts and Crafts Furniture: Shop of the Crafters at Cincinnati.* New York: Turn of the Century Editions, 1983.

Hageman, Jane Sikes. *Ohio Furniture Makers: 1790 to 1845.* Cincinnati, Ohio: Jane Sikes Hageman, 1984.

Miller, R. Craig. "Interior Design and Furniture." In *Design in America: The Cranbrook Vision, 1925–1950,* edited by Adele Westbrook and Anne Yarowsky. New York: Harry N. Abrams, Inc., in association with the Detroit Institute of Arts and the Metropolitan Museum of Art, 1983. Survey of Eliel Saarinen's furniture designs with the founding of the Cranbrook Academy of Art in 1932 and his influence as a teacher, particularly on his son Eero Saarinen, Florence Knoll, and Charles and Ray Eames. The book includes essays on the Cranbrook philosophy, staff, and history with excellent illustrations, documentation, and bibliographies of the main artists.

Pfeiffer, Bruce Brooks. *The Chairs of Frank Lloyd Wright.* New Haven: Yale University School of Architecture, 1987. Catalogue for an exhibition from November 2–20, 1987. Illustrations include rooms, with other furniture, drawings, and chairs. Introduction includes comments by many individuals concerned with studies about Wright.

Robertson, Cheryl. *The Domestic Scene (1897–1927): George M. Niedecken, Interior Architect.* Milwaukee: The Milwaukee Art Museum, 1981. Study of the life and work of one of Wright's major collaborators; offers a broad insight into the innovative concepts of the Chicago School.

Sikes, Jane E. *The Furniture Makers of Cincinnati, 1790 to 1849.* Cincinnati: Privately printed, 1976.

Spencer, Brian A., editor. *The Prairie School Tradition.* New York: Watson-Guptil Publications, 1979. Emphasis on buildings and related furniture.

Van Ravensway, Charles. *The Arts and Architecture of German Settlements in Missouri: A Survey of a Vanishing Culture.* Columbia: University of Missouri Press, 1979. Furniture discussed in chapter 13, pages 311–393, with the conclusion that colonists made very few objects in peasant traditions, some objects in simplified neoclassical designs, and many objects in vernacular and eclectic styles of the late 19th century; includes illustrations and bibliography.

Walters, Betty Lawson. *Furniture Makers of Indiana, 1793 to 1850.* Indianapolis: Indiana Historical Society, 1972.

REGIONAL SOURCES: New England

Churchill, Edwin A. *Simple Forms and Vivid Colors: An Exhibition of Maine Painted Furniture, 1800–1850, at the Maine State Museum, July 8, 1983, through February 28, 1984.* Augusta: The Maine State Museum, 1983.

Clunie, Margaret Burke; Farnam, Anne; and Trent, Robert F. *Furniture at the Essex Institute.* Salem, Massachusetts: The Essex Institute, 1980.

Connecticut Historical Society. "Connecticut Cabinetmakers up to 1820, Part I (A–L)." In *Connecticut Historical Society Bulletin* 32 (1967): 97–144. "Part II (L–W)" 33 (1968): 1–40.

Cooke, Edward S., Jr. *Fiddlebacks and Crooked-backs: Elijah Booth and Other Joiners in Newton and Woodbury, 1750–1820.* Waterbury, Connecticut: The Mattatuck Historical Society, 1982.

———. *Making Furniture in Preindustrial America: The Social Economy of Newton and Woodbury, Connecticut.* Baltimore, Maryland: Johns Hopkins University Press, 1996.

Fairbanks, Jonathan L., editor. *New England Begins: The Seventeenth Century.* 3 volumes. Boston: The Museum of Fine Arts, 1982. See Robert Blair St. George, " 'Set Thine House in Order': The Domestication of the Yeomanry in Seventeenth-Century New England," volume 2, pages 159–351, and Robert F. Trent, "New England Joinery and Turning before 1700," volume 3, pages 501–550.

Fales, Dean A., Jr. *Essex County Furniture: Documented Treasures from Local Collections, 1660–1860.* Salem, Massachusetts: The Essex Institute, 1965.

———. *The Furniture of Historic Deerfield.* New York: E. P. Dutton and Co., 1976. Includes 17th, 18th, and early-19th centuries.

Garvin, Donna-Belle; Garvin, James L.; and Page, John F. *Plain and Elegant, Rich and Common: Documented New Hampshire Furniture, 1750–1850.* Concord: New Hampshire Historical Society, 1979.

———. "Concord, New Hampshire: A Furniture-Making Capital." In *Historical New Hampshire* 45, no. 1 (Spring, 1990): 1–104. Catalogue of an exhibition at the New Hampshire Historical Society, 1990. Includes Deborah Tapley, compiler, "Furniture Craftsmen, Manufacturers, and Dealers Working in Concord, New Hampshire, prior to 1901."

Jobe, Brock, editor. *New England Furniture: Essays in Memory of Benno M. Forman.* Boston: The Society for the Preservation of New England Antiquities, 1987. Issued as Volume 72 of *Old Time New England.* Essays not superceded by later publications include Philip Zea on the Hadley chest, Gerald W. R. Ward on Connecticut 17th-century furniture, Jeanne Vibert Sloane on Newport furniture, Luke Bekerdite on carving in 18th-century Boston, Myrna Kaye on Maine furniture, and Robert D. Mussey, Jr., on historic furniture finishes.

———, and Kaye, Myrna, with the assistance of Philip Zea. *New England Furniture, the Colonial Era: Selections from the Society for the Preservation of New England Antiquities.* Boston: Houghton Mifflin, 1984.

———, editor. *Portsmouth Furniture: Masterworks from the New Hampshire Seacoast.* Boston: The Society for the Preservation of New England Antiquities, 1993. Furniture made locally or elsewhere and locally owned from the late-17th century to the early 19th; includes checklist of craftsmen by Kevin Shupe and illustrations of Portsmouth craftsmen brands by Kevin Nicholson, pages 423–438.

Kane, Patricia E. *Furniture of the New Haven Colony: The Seventeenth-Century Style.* New Haven: The New Haven Historical Society, 1973. Reprinted 1993 with Addendum.

Kenney, John Tarrant. *The Hitchcock Chair.* New York: C. N. Potter, 1971.

Labaree, Benjamin W., editor. *Samuel McIntire: A Bicentennial Symposium, 1757–1957.* Salem, Massachusetts: The Essex Institute, 1957. Essays by several authors on facets of McIntire's career and influence, including furniture and architectural carving; excellent bibliography to 1957 by Labaree.

Luther, Clair Franklin. *The Hadley Chest.* Hartford: Privately printed, 1935. For subsequent research, see Richard Lawrence Green, "Fertility Symbols on the Hadley Chests," *Antiques* 112 (August 1977): pages 250–257; Philip Zea in Jobe, *New England Furniture* in this section; and entry this section for Zea, Philip.

Maynard, Henry P., and Kirk, John T. *Connecticut Furniture: Seventeenth and Eighteenth Centuries.* Hartford: Wadsworth Atheneum, 1967. For recent research on New Haven Colony Furniture, see entry this section for Kane, Patricia E.

Moses, Michael. *Master Craftsmen of Newport: The Townsends and Goddards.* Tenafly, New Jersey: Michael Moses Americana Press and Israel Sack, Inc., 1984.

Mussey, Robert Haley, and Haley, Anne Rogers. "John Cogswell and Boston Bombé Furniture: Thirty-Five Years of Revolution in Politics and Design." In *American Furniture 1994,* pages 73–105. Nine examples of the bombé furniture form made from the early 1780s to the early 1790s attributed to Cogswell; other versions of the form categorized; documentation for No. 36 in this book.

Myers, Minor, Jr., and Mayhew, Edgar deN. *New London County Furniture, 1640–1840.* New London, Connecticut: The Lyman Allyn Museum, 1974. Background for No. 31 in this study.

Naeve, Milo M. "John [George] Glinn's Clock Case of 1750 for Henry Bromfield of Boston, Massachusetts." In *Furniture History,* XXVIII (1992), 22–34. Documentation for No. 26 in this book.

Page, John F. *Litchfield County Furniture, 1730–1850.* Litchfield, Connecticut: Litchfield Historical Society, 1969.

———. "Documented New Hampshire Furniture, 1750–1850." In *Antiques* 115 (1979): 1004–1015.

Richards, Nancy E. and Evans, Nancy Goyne with Cooper, Wendy and Podmaniczky, Michael S. and research assistance by Noyes, Clare G. *New England Furniture at Winterthur: Queen Anne and Chippendale Periods.* Winterthur, Delaware: The Henry Francis du Pont Winterthur Museum, 1997. In this book, documentation for Nos. 27, 28.

Robinson, Charles A. *Vermont Cabinetmakers and Chairmakers before 1855: A Checklist.* Shelburne, Vermont: Shelburne Museum, 1994. Includes essay by Philip Zea, "Craftsmen and Culture: An Introduction to Vermont Furniture Making."

St. George, Robert Blair. *The Wrought Covenant: Source Material for the Study of Craftsmen and Community in Southeastern New England, 1620–1700.* Brockton, Massachusetts: The Brockton Art Center and Fuller Memorial, 1979.

Sander, Penny J., editor, *Elegant Embellishments: Furnishings from New England Homes, 1660–1860.* Boston: The Society for the Preservation of New England Antiquities, 1982. Selections from SPNEA collections. For recent information about colonial furniture, see Jobe, Brock, et al., this section, *New England Furniture, the Colonial Era,* but the publication is the only compilation of the significant post-colonial furniture owned by the society (some made outside New England).

Trent, Robert F. *Folk Chairs of the Connecticut Coast, 1720–1840, as Viewed in the Light of Henry Focillon's Introdution to* Art Populaire. New Haven: The New Haven Colony Historical Society, 1977.

———. "The Endicott Chairs." In *Essex Institute Historical Collections,* 114, no. 2 (April 1978): pages 103–119. Documentation for No. 16 in this book with information about other Boston chairs from 1660 to 1695.

———, and Nelson, Nancy Lee. *New London County Joined Chairs, 1720–1790.* Hartford, Connecticut: The Connecticut Historical Society and the Lyman Allyn Museum, 1985. Catalogue for an exhibition at the Society and the Museum in 1985–1986. Issued as volume 50, No. 4 (Fall 1985) of *The Connecticut Historical Society Bulletin.*

Whitehill, Walter Muir, editor, assisted by Brock Jobe. *Boston Furniture of the Eighteenth Century.* Boston: The Colonial Society of Massachusetts, 1974. Reprinted 1986. Written by nine specialists, the book presents research resulting from a conference and exhibition organized by Jonathan L. Fairbanks on the organization of the furniture industry, forms, decoration, and woods; includes a checklist of craftsmen and a bibliography for individual craftsmen.

Zea, Philip. "Furniture." In *The Great River: Art & Society of the Connecticut Valley, 1635–1820*. Hartford: Wadsworth Atheneum, 1985.

———, and Flynt, Suzanne. *Hadley Chests*. Deerfield, Massachusetts: The Pocumtuck Valley Memorial Association, 1992. Catalogue for an exhibition at the Association, the Wadsworth Atheneum, and Israel Sack, Inc. Summarizes and includes new information not published by Zea, Philip in Jobe, Brock, editor, *New England Furniture* in this section.

———, and Dunlap, Donald. *The Dunlap Cabinetmakers: A Tradition in Craftsmanship*. Mechanicsburg, Pennsylvania: Stackpole Books, 1994. Includes measured drawings by John Nelson.

Zimmerman, Philip D., and Levy, Frank M. "An important block-front desk by Richard Walker of Boston." In *Antiques* 167 (1995): pages 436–441. Documentation for No. 29 in this book.

Zogry, Kenneth Joel. *The Best the Country Affords: Vermont Furniture, 1765–1850*. Bennington, Vermont: Bennington Museum, 1995.

REGIONAL SOURCES: South

Albright, Frank P. *Johann Ludwig Eberhardt and His Salem Clocks*. Winston-Salem, North Carolina: Old Salem, Inc., 1978.

Atlanta Historical Society. *Neat Pieces: The Plain-Style Furniture of 19th Century Georgia*. Atlanta: The Atlantic Historical Society, 1983.

[Bacot, H. Parrott.] *Southern Furniture and Silver: The Federal Period, 1788–1830*. Baton Rouge, Louisiana: The Anglo-American Art Museum of Louisiana State University, 1968.

Beasley, Ellen. "Tennessee Cabinetmakers and Chairmakers Through 1840." In *Antiques* 100 (1971): pages 612–621.

Beckerdite, Luke. "Architect-Designed Furniture in Eighteenth-Century Virginia: The Work of William Buckland and William Bernard Sears." In *American Furniture 1994*, pages 29–48.

Bennett, Swannee and Worthen, William B. *Arkansas Made: A Survey of the Decorative, Mechanical, and Fine Arts Produced in Arkansas, 1819–1870*. Volume One. Fayetteville, Arkansas, and London: The University of Arkansas Press, 1990. Furniture section includes "A Biographical Appendix of Arkansas Furnituremakers," pages 19–45, and "An Illustrated Catalogue of Arkansas Furniture," pages 46–80 (includes technical notes).

Bivins, John. *Furniture of Coastal North Carolina, 1700–1820*. Winston-Salem, North Carolina: The Museum of Early Southern Decorative Arts, 1988.

Elder, William Voss, III. *Baltimore Painted Furniture, 1800–1840*. Baltimore, Maryland: The Baltimore Museum of Art, 1972.

———, and Bartlett, Lu. *John Shaw: Cabinetmaker of Annapolis*. Baltimore, Maryland: The Baltimore Museum of Art, 1983. Excellent study of the foremost craftsman (1745–1829) in the capital; sixty-one objects traced to the shop.

Fitzgerald, Oscar P. *Green Family of Cabinetmakers: An Alexandria Institution 1817–1887*. Alexandria, Virginia: Alexandria Association, 1986.

Golovin, Ann Castrodale. "Cabinetmakers and Chairmakers of Washington, D.C., 1791–1840." In *Antiques* 107 (1975): pages 898–922.

Green, Henry D. *Furniture of the Georgia Piedmont Before 1830*. Atlanta: The High Museum of Art, 1976.

Gusler, Wallace B. *Furniture of Williamsburg and Eastern Virginia, 1710–1790*. Richmond: The Virginia Museum, 1979.

Hawes, Elaine. "Charles Koones and the Alexandria Furniture Trade, 1820–1860." Published as *Alexandria History* IX (1992). Includes checklist of cabinetmakers, Appendix 1.

Horton, Frank L. *The Museum of Early Southern Decorative Arts*. Winston-Salem, North Carolina: The Museum of Early Southern Decorative Arts, 1979. Furniture included in room views, illustrations of furniture, and in commentaries.

Hurst, Ronald L. and Prown, Jonathan. *Southern Furniture, 1680–1830: The Colonial Williamsburg Collection*. New York, New York: The Colonial Williamsburg Foundation in association with Harry N. Abrams, Inc., 1997.

Lohr, N. Gordon; Melchor, James R.; and Melchor, Marilyn S. *Eastern Shore, Virginia, Raised Panel Furniture, 1730–1830*. Norfolk: The Chrysler Museum, 1982.

North Carolina Museum of History. *North Carolina Furniture*. Raleigh: The North Carolina Museum of History, 1977.

Page, Addison Franklin. *Kentucky Furniture*. Louisville: The J. B. Speed Art Museum, 1974.

Piorkowski, Patricia Ann. *Piedmont Virginia Furniture: The Product of Provincial Cabinetmakers*. Lynchburg, Virginia: Lynchburg Museum System, 1982.

Poesch, Jessie J. *The Art of the Old South: Painting, Sculpture, Architecture & the Products of Craftsmen, 1560–1860*. New York: Alfred A. Knopf, 1983. Documented and illustrated survey, with excellent bibliography, that includes furniture.

———. *Early Furniture of Louisiana, 1750–1830*. New Orleans: The Louisiana State Museum, 1972.

Weidman, Gregory R. *Furniture in Maryland, 1740–1940: The Collection of the Maryland Historical Society*. Baltimore: The Maryland Historical Society, 1984. Technical notes, essays, and illustrations; emphasis on furniture made in Maryland, but includes furniture made elsewhere.

———, and Goldsborough, Jennifer F., et al. *Classical Maryland, 1815–1845: Fine and Decorative Arts from the Golden Age*. Baltimore: Maryland Historical Society, Museum, and Library of Maryland History, 1993. Catalogue for an exhibition, 1993. Furniture emphasis.

Whitley, Mrs. Wade Hampton (Edna Talbott). *A Checklist of Kentucky Cabinetmakers from 1775 to 1859*. Paris, Kentucky: Privately Printed, 1970.

Williams, Derita Coleman, and Harsh, Nathan. *The Art and Mystery of Tennessee Furniture and Its Makers Through 1850*. Nashville: The Tennessee Historical Society and the Tennessee State Museum Foundation, 1988. Color illustrations; checklist of craftsmen through 1850.

Winters, Robert E., editor. *North Carolina Furniture, 1700–1900*. Raleigh: The North Carolina Museum of History, Division of Archives and History, Department of Cultural Resources, 1977. See Bivans, John, this section, for later study of coastal furniture.

REGIONAL SOURCES: Southwest

Pierce, Donna. "Furniture." In *Spanish New Mexico: The Colonial Arts Society*. Donna Pierce and Marta Weigle editors. Santa Fe: Museum of New Mexico Press, 1996. Volume I, pages 61–71. Discussion and color illustrations of seventy-three examples, mainly from New Mexico but also from other Spanish cultures collected for comparison with local furniture; well documented; major collection.

Steinfeldt, Cecilia, and Stover, Donald. *Early Texas Furniture and Decorative Arts*. San Antonio: The San Antonio Museum Association, [1973].

Taylor, Lonn, and Bokides, Dessa, Introduction by Jonathan L. Fairbanks. *New Mexican Furniture, 1600–1940: The Origins, Survival, and Revival of Furniture Making in the Hispanic Southwest*. Santa Fe: Museum of New Mexico Press, 1987. Documented survey; excellent illustrations, many in color, authoritative.

Vedder, Alan C. *Furniture of Spanish New Mexico*. Santa Fe: Sunstone Press, 1977. For information about the background and types, see above Taylor, Lonn and Bokides, Dessa; however, this book includes privately-owned furniture not illustrated elsewhere.

REGIONAL SOURCES: West

Cooke, Edward S., Jr. "Scandinavian Modern Furniture in the Arts and Crafts Period: The Collaboration of the Greenes and the Halls." In *American Furniture 1993*, pages 55–74.

Jones, Harvey L. *California Woodworking: An Exhibition of Contemporary Handcrafted Furniture*. Oakland: The Oakland Museum, 1980.

Maloof, Sam. *Sam Maloof: Woodworker*. Introduction by Jonathan L. Fairbanks. Tokyo: Kodansha International Ltd., 1983. Autobiography with illustrations of furniture and procedures.

Morningstar, Connie. *Early Utah Furniture*. Logan: Utah State University Press, 1976.

Trapp, Kenneth R., et al. *The Arts and Crafts Movement in California: Living the Good Life*. New York: The Oakland Museum and Abbeville Press, 1993. Catalogue for an exhibition at the Oakland Museum, The Renwick Gallery of the National Museum of American Art, Smithsonian Institution, 1993–1994. Furniture included with other decorative arts in essays by Trapp about San Francisco, Leslie Greene Bowman about Southern California, and Bruce Kamerling about San Diego; includes biographies of craftsmen and company histories by Trapp and Kim Cooper; selective bibliography.

INDEX

Bold face references are to page numbers; others are to illustrations. Craftsmen, designers and manufacturers are included. Forms are selectively represented. Motifs are cited by major interpretations in differing periods. Styles are easily located through the table of contents, and the reader is advised to consult commentaries pertinent to an inquiry.

W, Y, Z